DEVELOPMENTAL

CHARACTERISTICS

Other books in this series:
  Developmental Therapy,
    Mary M. Wood, editor (University Park Press, 1975)
  Music in Developmental Therapy,
    Jennie Purvis and Shelley Samet, editors (University Park Press, 1976)
  Developmental Art Therapy,
    Geraldine H. Williams and Mary M. Wood, authors (University Park Press, 1977)

DEVELOPMENTAL THERAPY FOR YOUNG CHILDREN WITH AUTISTIC CHARACTERISTICS

by
Ann W. Bachrach
Therapist and Parent Worker at Oak Tree
Children's Center
Albany, Georgia
Ada R. Mosley
Therapist and Parent Worker, Rutland Center
Athens, Georgia
Faye L. Swindle
Coordinator, Rutland Center Autistic Project
Athens, Georgia
and
Mary M. Wood
Professor of Special Education, University of
Georgia
and
Director of Training, Rutland Center
Athens, Georgia

 UNIVERSITY PARK PRESS
BALTIMORE

UNIVERSITY PARK PRESS
International Publishers in Science and Medicine
233 East Redwood Street
Baltimore, Maryland 21202

Copyright © 1978 by University Park Press (Part 5 excluded)

Typeset by The Composing Room of Michigan, Inc.

Manufactured in the United States of America by Collins Lithographing and
Printing Co., Inc.

Library of Congress Cataloging in Publication Data
Main entry under title:

Developmental therapy for young children with autistic
characteristics

Bibliography: p.
Includes index.
1.   Mentally ill children—Education.   2.   Autism.
3.   Developmental psychology.   I.   Bachrach, Ann W.
[DNLM: 1.   Autism—In infancy and childhood.
2.   Autism—Therapy.   3.   Psychotherapy—In infancy
and childhood.   WM203 D489]
LC4169.D48   371.9′2   77-16370
ISBN 0-8391-1186-X

Contents

Preface

For a foundation in general applications of Developmental Therapy, the reader is encouraged to use the basic text, *Developmental Therapy*. This treatment program grew out of work done at the Rutland Center, Athens, Georgia, by Mary M. Wood of the University of Georgia. Developmental Therapy had its beginnings as a demonstration psychoeducational program of community-based services for severely emotionally disturbed, including autistic, young children and their families. It was initiated in 1970 through the cooperative effort of the local school system, the community health center, the University of Georgia, the Georgia Division of Mental Health, the Georgia Department of Education, and the Bureau of Education for the Handicapped, U.S. Office of Education.

The learning experiences contained in Part 5 of this text were developed and pilot-tested with children enrolled in the Stage One Developmental Therapy classes at the Rutland Center, Dr. J. C. Mullis, Director, and were supported in part by a Title VI grant from the Georgia Department of Education, 1975–1976.

Developmental Therapy, the approach upon which the curriculum in this book builds, is fully described in the following sources:

Wood, M. M. (ed.). 1975. Developmental Therapy. University Park Press, Baltimore.

Wood, M. M. (ed.). 1972. The Rutland Center Model for Treating Emotionally Disturbed Children. Eric No. ED 087703. Rutland Center Technical Assistance Office, Athens, Georgia.

Purvis, J., and Samet, S. (eds.) 1976. Music in Developmental Therapy. University Park Press, Baltimore.

Williams, G. H., and Wood, M. M. 1977. Developmental Art Therapy. University Park Press, Baltimore.

Acknowledgments

The authors would like to recognize the contribution of the following individuals in preparing the home programs and learning experiences contained in Parts 3 and 5:

Karen Davis
Rey Martin
Sarah McGinley
Susan Norton
Amy Rogers
Phyliss Stoneman
Geraldine Williams
Sarah J. Wood

The text of this book was prepared under the editorial supervision of Michael Hendrick, Information Officer, Developmental Therapy Institute, University of Georgia, and Melissa Behm, Production Editor, University Park Press.

Dedication

Because they have taught us to listen and to look,
to understand when there are no spoken words,
Because they have been the motivating force,
We gratefully dedicate this work to the children and their families.

Who Can Benefit From This Curriculum?

Well, anybody! The curriculum is fun, arousing, and simple, yet stimulating. Any children who are developmentally delayed—no matter what the cause—can benefit from this kind of developmentally targeted experience. The techniques and materials are appropriate for many kinds of children.

The program described in this text includes samples of techniques and materials, routines and environments, activity periods, learning experiences, and home programs designed specifically for the young autistic child, functioning developmentally from birth to three years regardless of chronological age. A few of the learning experiences apply to children developmentally between three and five years. The program can be used by parents as well as by teachers and day care workers.

The Developmental Therapy approach to dealing with young autistic children involves an intense, pleasurable experience using all sensory channels to communicate that the world can be a joyful place. It is an attempt to respond to each child as frequently and consistently as possible in order to provide an environment that is pleasurable and stimulating. This is necessary to arouse and move children forward from Stage One through normal developmental sequences.

The Developmental Therapy experience is especially suited for the child who is functioning well below his age expectancy level and who does not seem to be responding, learning, or developing. Such a child may be "unaware" of his environment; consequently, he receives little pleasure from it. He may not seem to know you are there, may not be able to talk, and yet, somehow, you know his understanding is greater than his responses. Body rocking, walking in circles, or twirling objects takes up most of his time. Such disorganized behavior prevents him from seeing what is going on in the room. He may scream or cover his ears when you talk. He may be that one child who is a mystery to you. Nothing you try seems to work.

But the task at hand is not to dwell on a child's deficits. It is to awaken and mobilize every aspect of functioning. Then, when a child is aware and responses begin to flow spontaneously, the task is to redirect those responses into organized, pleasure-producing results. These results lead to the accomplishment of the overall goal for Stage One children in Developmental Therapy: *responding to the environment with pleasure*.

DEVELOPMENTAL THERAPY FOR YOUNG CHILDREN WITH AUTISTIC CHARACTERISTICS

part **1**

AN INTRODUCTION TO THE PROGRAM

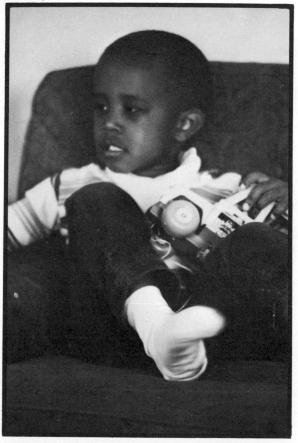

CHARACTERISTICS OF AUTISTIC, CSID CHILDREN[1]

There is a small group of severely handicapped children for whom regular special education programs generally have proved less than effective. Depending upon who has made the diagnosis, these children have been labeled as *schizophrenic, aphasic-apraxic, autistic, trainable mentally retarded, severely learning-disabled, severely multihandicapped, severely language-delayed, sensory-disordered, Heller's syndrome,* and/or *neurologically and perceptually disordered.* While such a collection of labels may be confusing, there seems to be some agreement on the characteristics of the children themselves: Creak (1964), Kuglemass (1970), the National Society for Autistic Children (1973), Rimland (1964), Ruttenberg and Wolf (1967), Rutter (1970), Schopler (1965), Treffert (1970), and others have contributed abundantly to the current knowledge about the characteristics of such children and their families. In a review of such studies, cross-referencing characteristics from many sources, the Rutland Center CSID staff agreed upon a nine-point list, adapted from that of the National Society for Autistic Children, as the basis for identifying such children. These identifying characteristics are:

1. Severely nonfunctional speech or complete lack of speech
2. Unusual reaction to perceptual stimuli, such as seeming not to hear certain sounds and over-reacting to others (e.g., holding hands over ears or "looking through" objects), poor eye contact, or inability to perform certain gross and/or fine motor activities (e.g., walking with peculiar gait, limpness in fingers, inability to hold a pencil appropriately)

3. Extreme distress for no discernible reason because of minor changes in the environment
4. Lack of intellectual development or retardation in certain areas, sometimes accompanied by normal or superior abilities in other areas
5. Repetitive and peculiar use of toys and objects in an inappropriate manner and/or similar repetitive and peculiar body motions, such as incessant rocking
6. Impaired or complete lack of relatedness; social inaccessibility to children, parents, and adults
7. Onset of disorder at birth or apparent normal early development followed by deterioration in functioning
8. Hyperactivity or passivity
9. Apparent insensitivity to pain

The children for whom this curriculum was developed are those with severely nonfunctional speech (characteristic no. 1), unusual reaction to perceptual stimuli (characteristic no. 2), and at least two other characteristics from the list. The severity of such characteristics may range from mild to severe; however, even the presence of these characteristics in mild forms becomes significant when in combination. When four such characteristics are present, the result is almost always a significant impairment in all aspects of the developmental process.

It appears that all CSID children have unique sensory deficits; they seem to lack the quality to make *meaning* from sensory stimulation rather than to lack the ability to receive sensory stimulation. Such a deficit produces the phenomenon of "autistic aloneness," and a vicious, downward cycle begins. Lack of meaning results in lack of suitable responses. Inappropriate responses evoke distorted responses from significant people around the child. The result is a multideficit child whose developmental progress is arrested or fragmented. Characterized by unusual patterns of skills and deficits, such a child is often denied the essential, human experience of close relationships with others. His skills for social exchange and interpersonal communication do not develop adequately, and the resulting aloneness compounds the problems associated with developmental lags.

It is the underlying premise of this curriculum guide that *intervention, based on sequential devel-*

---

[1]The bylaws of the National Society for Autistic Children (NSAC, 1976) state that the term *autistic children* identifies children exhibiting "infantile autism, autistic-like behavior, childhood schizophrenia, or other profound behavioral and/or communicative disorders." At the Rutland Center such children are identified as CSID, or those with severe communication and sensory integrative disorders. For this reason, they are referred to in this text as CSID children. Those who specialize in working with CSID children at the Rutland Center are referred to as the CSID staff.

opmental objectives, has the potential of helping the CSID child begin to experience relationships, social experiences, satisfying behavior patterns, and communication processes that help him to develop concepts, to abstract, and, subsequently, to begin ordering his world of confusion. By incorporating experiences into a broadly based developmental curriculum the child can be assisted in obtaining meaning from sensory inputs and can begin to see, hear, feel, speak, and respond with understanding.

INCIDENCE

In a five-year period, 43 children with CSID (i.e., autistic) characteristics have been identified and served at the Rutland Center and at nine similar centers in Georgia.[2] These centers are available to a total child population of 411,464 children to age 14. If this is a representative sample, the prevalence rate of CSID/autistic characteristics is 0.01% among the child population. Compare this figure with others reported in the literature. Lotter's (1967) study of 87,000 English children (ages 8–10) reported 32 children with similar characteristics, an incidence of 0.04%. In contrast, Ritvo et al. (1971) identified 74 children (12 years of age or younger) in a retrospective study of UCLA Neuropsychiatric Institute records from 1969–1970. The hospital served a total population of 6,030,051. However, the smaller prevalence rate of 0.0012% in this study is not comparable because the population figure includes adults. Wing (1974) offers a 0.05% prevalence figure and projects an estimate of three to five children with autistic characteristics in every 10,000 children. The conclusion is that the definitions of CSID children are so varied that estimates of the number of severely handicapped children with CSID characteristics are quite divergent; nevertheless, these characteristics represent a profoundly debilitating condition and make up a distinct subset of the severely handicapped population.

---

[2]Results of a survey by Dr. W. W. Swan conducted in 1975 at the University of Georgia.

Using Wing's ratio, there are possibly 24,925 CSID children between the ages of 5 and 18 in the United States, each needing a highly specialized program. At the present time, there are too few programs offering appropriate services of any kind for these CSID, or autistic-like, children. There are few teacher-training institutions that offer courses specifically to train parents and professionals. Yet parents and professional personnel recognize the need for highly specific techniques, activities, and materials for educating these children in school and at home. It is for these parents and professionals that this text has been prepared.

THE THERAPEUTIC PROCESS

In this program, CSID (i.e., autistic) children are viewed from a developmental perspective. Normal developmental guidelines have been combined with psychoeducational procedures to form a curriculum called Developmental Therapy. This curriculum may be used by all who are associated with a child, including professional staff, parents, and day care workers or school teachers.

No child is rejected from service because of the severity of his problem. In using the Developmental Therapy model with these children, the staff also have involved parents actively in the treatment program by using them as co-teachers at home and at the center (Schopler and Reichler, 1971). This opens a great number of possibilities for meeting the needs of these children and their parents.

A basic assumption of Developmental Therapy is the existence of normal traits within every child. While a child may have severe, autistic characteristics, he also has normal developmental characteristics that need to be utilized in treatment. One strategy to strengthen the development of these traits is to provide the child with appropriate opportunities to see other, more normal children and to model their behavior in progressive steps. Thus, to progress in an optimal manner, every child needs normal experiences in addition to a therapeutic program. Recognizing the existence of this need even among the most severely impaired, the staff at the Rutland

Center emphasize concurrent placement in other child-serving programs while the child is participating in the intensive, highly specialized program at the center.

Referrals

Most referrals of CSID children probably come from child-serving agencies other than the public school system. In general, referrals come directly from parents, early childhood development programs, training centers for the moderately to severely retarded, public health facilities, and speech and hearing clinics.

Before a referred child is enrolled, he will be involved in three processes: *screening, intake,* and *staffing.* These processes provide three decision points between referral and treatment, at any one of which a child can be directed to another resource or program if he does not appear to have CSID characteristics as defined above. After referral, a child is given a series of evaluations—developmental, educational, psychological, and psychiatric. Information from all other available sources is also used to determine if the child is in need of the CSID services that the Rutland Center provides.

Children accepted for the program are enrolled in a Rutland Center Developmental Therapy class with other children who are at the same developmental level (no more than six children per group). These intensive Developmental Therapy classes are conducted five days per week, at least two hours per day. Following the group experience, each child should receive two additional programs daily. The first involves him with his parents once each day in a structured, therapeutic activity, and the second is a parallel school experience.

Parent Involvement

Test results, records of child progress, and current program materials are shared with all parents. Parents are encouraged to play a maximal role in the child's treatment program, some even feeling comfortable enough to work in the Developmental Therapy classrooms. Nevertheless, children are accepted for service even with a minimal commitment from the parent.

Because of the severe developmental deficits of these children, specific programs to assist their parents in teaching self-help and family and home routines are usually necessary. The following experiences are made available for parents and children according to the needs and skills of each family:

1. *Observation:* Parents may learn about the program by observing the class through a one-way mirror with staff who also are working with the child. For many parents, observing may be their first opportunity to actually see their child interacting successfully in a group situation. Observation may be of help to a parent who wants to see a particular objective or activity being implemented. Also, observation provides parents with the opportunity to really know what is going on in their child's program.

2. *Specific Skill Development Program for Parents:* Parents may seek training in specific management procedures. The amount and the duration of each training activity depend on the needs and skills of the parents and child. A typical parent training sequence may be as follows:

   a. Teacher demonstrates an activity (selected by parent and teacher) that relates to one or more Developmental Therapy objectives. Parent observes teacher and child with the activity. A second staff member observes with the parent to point out certain therapy techniques essential in teaching the child this activity.

   b. Parent takes activity (outlined by staff) home to practice. Parent will be instructed to teach activities daily at a certain time and place in the way decided upon by the staff and parent in order to get maximal response. A daily log will be kept by the parent to show progress.

   c. Parent demonstrates skill in conducting activity at biweekly sessions at the Rutland Center with the teacher and the other staff person.

3. *Field Experiences:* Parents often find it difficult to take these children out in public. Outings may result in stress and embarrassment to the par-

ents. When this situation exists, a program of field trips can be planned by the teacher and parent.

Such a program might include visits to restaurants, grocery stores, and department stores. During these experiences, emphasis is placed on helping the parent set limits and on learning how to manage the child's unpredictable behavior.

4. *Home Programs:*[3] Very often the presence of a CSID child in a home makes it extremely difficult for the family to maintain or even develop a routine. The teacher might begin by participating with the family in routines, eventually assisting them in planning and establishing routines beneficial to both the child and his family.

The teacher also will demonstrate and then assist the parents in teaching their child specific activities necessary for home routines. These activities should be mutually determined by the parent and teacher and might include such experiences as eating, bathing, dressing, bedtime, involvement in various family activities, discipline, and preparing simple food.

Group meetings among all family members could be organized by the teacher. Important extended family members might be included also. Topics to work on might include helping other family members explore ways they can more helpfully interact with the child, especially during play and leisure times.

PARALLEL SCHOOL EXPERIENCES

Frequently children with severe CSID characteristics may not be involved in any school program at the time of referral. Some of these children may not be ready for enrollment in another school. The staff is responsible for finding an appropriate school placement for each child as soon as possible. The child's Developmental Therapy program should not be isolated from other forms of daily school life, and, through close linkage of the educational environments, carry-over

should be greatly enhanced from the center class to the parallel school placement.

The major goal of the parallel school program is to provide successful peer experiences for CSID children with children of higher developmental stages in less intensive programs than the Developmental Therapy classes or the individualized programs with their parents.

Collaboration between the two settings seems to be most effective when the child's Developmental Therapy teacher also teams with the teacher in the parallel school, or vice versa, and they teach together.

DEVELOPMENTAL THERAPY CURRICULUM AND CLASSES: WHAT IS THE CURRICULUM AND HOW DOES IT WORK?[4]

Developmental Therapy is designed for special education or early childhood teachers, mental health workers, parents, volunteers, and paraprofessionals using the therapeutic classroom setting with five to eight children in a group. *It is a treatment process that 1) does not isolate the handicapped child from the mainstream of normal experiences, 2) uses normal changes in development as a means to expedite the therapeutic process, 3) uses normal sequences of development to guide the therapeutic process, and 4) has an evaluation system as a part of the therapeutic process.*

The basic curriculum areas of Developmental Therapy are: Behavior, Communication, Socialization, and (Pre)Academics. Within each of these areas there is a series of measurably stated developmental objectives which are sequenced into five stages of therapy.

The curriculum provides a broad outline to guide the teacher in planning appropriate experience sequences for the handicapped child. Five standards were used in constructing the curriculum:

1. The curriculum is broad enough to cover any serious emotional or behavioral problems seen in the young disturbed or autistic child.

---

[3]Part 3 contains samples of several home programs prepared for use in children's homes by parents and CSID staff.

[4]From Wood, M. M. (ed.). 1975. Developmental Therapy. University Park Press, Baltimore.

2. The curriculum provides for sequences of experiences that stimulate growth and utilize new skills as they spontaneously emerge in the child.
3. The curriculum is adaptable to individual differences but also effective in a group setting.
4. The curriculum is general enough to allow for clinical inference and for parent and teacher judgments, yet specific enough to provide for objective evaluation.
5. The curriculum is not dependent upon a child's verbal or cognitive ability.

A summary of Stages I–IV is given below. Stage V does not fall within the scope of this study and therefore has been omitted.

EVALUATION

The program evaluation system is composed of both formative and summative phases and is criterion-referenced to Developmental Therapy. There are three specific evaluative measures (Huberty, Quirk, and Swan, 1973).

One measure of child progress is determined by obtaining the average percentage of Developmental Therapy objectives mastered by children from the time of enrollment and at five-week intervals until termination or at the end of the school year. (Use the Developmental Therapy Objectives Rating Form (DTORF); see Appendix b). The numerical summaries can yield pre-post measures of mastery of

---

Stage I:
Responding to the Environment
with Pleasure

Parents' and Teacher's Roles:	Arouser and satisfier of basic needs
Techniques:	Body language; controlled vocabulary; routine; stimulating activities
Intervention:	Constant physical contact, caring, arousing
Environment and Experiences:	Routine constant, luring rather than demanding; stimulating, arousing sensory activities

Stage II:
Responding to the Environment
with Success

Parents' and Teacher's Roles:	Verbal reflector of success; redirector of old coping behaviors to successful outcomes
Techniques:	Routine; consistency; holding limits; verbal reflection
Intervention:	Frequent, both physical and verbal
Environment and Experiences:	Activities leading to self-confidence; communication activities; success; free and structured play time

Stage III:
Applying Individual Skill
to Group Procedure

Parents' and Teacher's Roles:	Reflector of feelings and progress; encourager; holder of limits
Techniques:	Reflection of feelings; predictability; frequent verbal intervention; consistency
Intervention:	Frequent; group focus, mostly verbal
Environment and Experiences:	Focus on rules; the group; consequences; sharing; approximates real life

Stage IV:
Investing in
Group Processes

Parents' and Teacher's Roles:	Reflector of reality and success; counselor; group leader
Techniques:	Reflection; Life Space Interviewing (LSI); interpretation; group planning and discussion for problem solving
Intervention:	Intermittent, approximating real life
Environment and Experiences:	Normal expectations; role play; emphasis on learning; field trips

objectives by individual children or by groups of children (averages) (Swan and Wood, 1975).

A second measure of child progress is an observational instrument, the Systematic Who-to-Whom Analysis Notation (SWAN) based on subsets of the Developmental Therapy objectives. This instrument is used by program evaluators to collect information relative to the child's overt behavior. SWAN data are collected during the second, third, eighth, and ninth weeks of each 10-week treatment period. Pre-post comparisons of these data are also possible (Swan, 1971).

A third measure of child progress is the Referral Form Checklist (RFCL), composed of 54 behaviorally stated problems used as a pre-post measure to obtain teachers' and parents' perceptions of the child's problems at the time of intake and again at termination. The RFCL is used also to assess the child's status at one year after termination (Wood, 1972).

AN ILLUSTRATION OF CHILD PROGRESS

Table 1 presents a sample DTORF Summary for one five-year-old CSID child. The child was rated after he had attended the Developmental Therapy class for eight days (9/20/76). This provided the baseline. Subsequently he was rated every five weeks. The dot (·) indicates an objective mastered.[5] An X indicates an objective selected to be a treatment focus. As seen in this summary, the child made steady progress in Behavior and (Pre)Academics. His progress in Socialization was uneven: he moved ahead in some objectives and showed no progress in others. In Communication he made some progress early in treatment, then apparently lost these gains several months later. Such uneven patterns of acceleration and regression seem to be somewhat characteristic of CSID children. This summary also illustrates the relatively long period of time needed for some CSID children to develop functional speech.[6]

---

[5]The numerals correspond to the Developmental Therapy objectives contained in Appendix a.

[6]A simplified version of this record-keeping system is contained in Appendix c as a part of the format for an individualized education program (IEP), which is required under P.L. 94-142.

To further illustrate the uneven development patterns and heterogenous characteristics of CSID children, consider the following data on 11 CSID children enrolled in Developmental Therapy Stage One classes.

The children ranged in age from 2 years, 11 months to 5 years, 10 months when they entered the Developmental Therapy program. All 11 had severely nonfunctional speech or complete lack of speech, and all displayed unusual reactions to perceptual stimuli. Three of the 11 children showed extreme distress for no discernable reason, four were extremely hyperactive or passive, and six had a history of apparent normal early development followed by deterioration in function. Of the 11, six evidenced lack of intellectual development in certain areas but possessed normal abilities in other areas. Six also exhibited repetitive and peculiar use of toys and objects, and six showed a significantly impaired ability to relate to adults, parents, and other children.

When rated after eight days in the program for a developmental baseline on the Developmental Therapy Objectives Rating Form (DTORF), one child rated at Stage Two in Communication. All the other children rated at Stage One in each of the four curriculum areas: Behavior, Communication, Socialization, and (Pre)Academics. However, there were strengths evident among the 11 children, as reflected in the number of objectives mastered at the time of each child's entry into the program. Table 2 outlines selected objectives and the number of children who had mastered each objective at entry when the DTORF baseline rating was done. It is interesting that S-1 (to be aware of others) was the most frequently mastered objective at entry and the only one mastered by more than half of the 11. It is important to note however, that this objective does not require that the child's awareness be direct or positive. Table 2 also shows that, consistently, the lower order objectives were more frequently mastered at entry than were the higher order objectives.

As these 11 children progressed, their rates for mastering objectives reflected uneven, widely differing patterns of development. Table 3 illustrates this point, showing the number of weeks of treatment that elapsed from entry to mastery of the same selected objectives listed in Table 2.

It is difficult to see a sequential pattern for each

Table 1. Sample DTORF Summary

Name: _____

Behavior

Date	Stage I							Stage II					Stage III							Stage IV					Stage V	
10th wk ( )																										
5th wk ( )																										
10th wk ( )																										
5th wk ( )																										
10th wk ( )																										
5th wk ( )																										
10th wk ( )																										
5th wk (4-28-77)	·	·	·	·	·	·	·	·	·	X	X															
10th wk (3-18-77)	·	·	·	·	·	·	·	·	·	X	X															
5th wk (2-11-77)	·	·	·	·	·	·	·	·	·	·	X															
10th wk (11-1-76)	·	·	·	·	·	·	·	X	X	X	X															
5th wk (10-13-76)	·	·	·	X	X	X	X	X																		
Baseline (9-20-76)	·	·	·	·	·	X	X	·																		
Objectives	0 1	2	3	4	5	6	7	8	9	10	11	12	13	14	15	16	17	18	19	20	21	22	23	24	25	26

Communication

Date	Stage I							Stage II					Stage III							Stage IV					Stage V		
10th wk ( )																											
5th wk ( )																											
10th wk ( )																											
5th wk ( )																											
10th wk ( )																											
5th wk ( )																											
10th wk ( )																											
5th wk (4-28-77)	·	·	·	·	·	X	X	X	X	·	X																
10th wk (3-18-77)	·	·	·	·	·	X	X	X	·	X	·	X															
5th wk (2-11-77)	·	·	·	·	X	·	X	X	X	X	X																
10th wk (11-1-76)	·	·	·	·	·	·	X	X	X	·	X	·	X														
5th wk (10-13-76)	·	·	·	·	·	·	·	X	X	X	X																
Baseline (9-20-76)	·	·	·	·	·	X	·	X	X																		
Objectives	0 1	2	3	4	5	6	7	8	9	10	11	12	13	14	15	16	17	18	19	20	21	22	23	24	25 26	27 28	29 30

· = Mastery   X = Short term goal

Unmarked spaces indicate that the child is not ready to begin work on these objectives.

(Continued)

Table 1. (continued) Sample DTORF Summary

Socialization

Date	Stage I												Stage II						Stage III						Stage IV						Stage V
10th wk ( )																															
5th wk ( )																															
10th wk ( )																															
5th wk ( )																															
10th wk ( )																															
5th wk ( )																															
10th wk ( )																															
5th wk (4-24-77)	·	·	·	·	·	·	·	·	X	X	·	·	·	·	·	·	X	X													
10th wk (3-18-77)	·	·	·	·	·	·	·	·	·	·	·	·	·	·	X	·	X	X													
5th wk (2-11-77)	·	·	·	·	·	·	·	·	X	·	·	·	·	·	X	·	X														
10th wk (11-17-76)	·	·	·	·	·	·	·	·	X	·	·	·	X	X	·	·	X														
5th wk (10-13-76)	·	·	·	·	·	·	·	·	·	·	·	X	X	X	X																
Baseline (9-20-76)	·	·	·	·	X	·	·	·	X	X	X	·																			
Objectives	1	2	3	4	5	6	7	8	9	10	11	12	13	14	15	16	17	18	19	20	21	22	23	24	25	26	27	28	29	30	31

(Pre)Academic

Date	Stage I																	Stage II													
10th wk ( )																															
5th wk ( )																															
10th wk ( )																															
5th wk ( )																															
10th wk ( )																															
5th wk ( )																															
10th wk ( )																															
5th wk (4-24-77)	·	·	·	·	·	·	·	·	·	·	·	·	·	·	·	·	·	·	·	·	·	·	·	·	·	·	·	X	X	X	X
10th wk (3-18-77)	·	·	·	·	·	·	·	·	·	·	·	·	·	·	·	·	·	·	·	X	·	X	·	·	X	·	·	X			
5th wk (2-11-77)	·	·	·	·	·	·	·	·	·	·	·	·	·	·	·	·	·	·	·	X	·	X	·	X	X						
10th wk (11-17-76)	·	·	·	·	·	·	·	·	·	·	·	·	·	·	·	·	·	·	X	X	·	·	·	·	X	X	·				
5th wk (10-13-76)	·	·	·	·	·	·	·	·	·	·	·	X	·	·	·	·	·	X	X	X	·										
Baseline (9-20-76)	·	·	·	·	·	·	·	X	·	·	·	X	·	·	·	·	X	X													
Objectives	1	2	3	4	5	6	7	8	9	10	11	12	13	14	15	16	17	18	19	20	21	22	23	24	25	26	27	28	29	30	31

(Pre)Academic (continued)

Date	Stage III																	Stage IV				Stage V					
10th wk ( )																											
5th wk ( )																											
10th wk ( )																											
5th wk ( )																											
10th wk ( )																											
5th wk ( )																											
10th wk ( )																											
5th wk (4-24-77)																											
10th wk (3-18-77)																											
5th wk (2-11-77)																											
10th wk (11-17-76)																											
5th wk (10-13-76)																											
Baseline (9-20-76)																											
Objectives	32	33	34	35	36	37	38	39	40	41	42	43	44	45	46	47	48	49	50	51	52	53	54	55	56	57	

· = Mastery   X = Short term goal

Unmarked spaces indicate that the child is not ready to begin work on these objectives.

Table 2. Developmental Therapy objectives mastered at time of entry (baseline) by 11 CSID children

	Objectives	Number of children
Behavior	B-4 to respond with motor and body responses to complex environmental and verbal stimuli	5
	B-5 to actively assist in learning self-help skills	4
	B-6 to respond independently to several play materials	3
	B-7 to indicate recall of classroom routine by moving spontaneously without physical stimulus	1
	B-8 to use play materials appropriately	0
Communication	C-4 to voluntarily use recognizable single-word approximations	2
	C-7 to produce a meaningful, recognizable sequence of words	1
	C-11 to use simple word sequences to command or request	0
Socialization	S-1 to be aware of others	8
	S-6 to respond to adult's requests to come	3
	S-15 to initiate appropriate minimal movement toward another child	0
(Pre)Academics	A-5 to respond with rudimentary fine and gross motor skills to manipulative tasks associated with 24 months	5
	A-6 to imitate simple, familiar actions of adult	3
	A-28 to discriminate concepts of differences	0

individual child, especially in the area of Behavior. Some of the higher order objectives were mastered in less time than some of the lower order objectives. It also seems evident that progress in the selected Communication and Socialization objectives was generally slower than in Behavior and (Pre)Academics. Finally, when comparing children's progress, it becomes evident that some children made more rapid progress on these particular objectives than did other children.

Such information can only leave us with a sense of the unique patterns of development in each of these CSID children and a need to know more about this disability. One obvious question is whether or not the autistic, CSID syndrome is a particular condition or a cluster of problems affecting each child's development in a special way. Another question concerns identifying characteristics that might be evident at entry and predictive of what rate of progress can be expected. These questions are only a few of the many to be studied. In the meantime, careful, systematic collection of such developmental data can indicate to parents and teachers the pattern and rate of growth of the individual child.

Table 3. Number of weeks to mastery of selected Developmental Therapy objectives

Objective	Child										
	1	2	3	4	5	6	7	8	9	10	11
B-4	10	10	15	45	(30)	5	BL	BL	25	145	10
B-5	35	(35)	(50)	50	(30)	BL	BL	30	60	145	20
B-6	30	30	5	60	BL	35	5	5	80	150	BL
B-7	5	5	20	55	(30)	35	5	5	25	135	10
B-8	(60)	(30)	(40)	(45)	(30)	55	10	(50)	80	(135)	35
C-4	(75)	35	(55)	(80)	(30)	30	BL	10	BL	145	5
C-7		(5)		(5)		(35)	30	35	55	140	25
C-11							(25)	(20)	130	(5)	75
S-1	BL	BL	BL	10	BL	BL	BL	BL	40	BL	5
S-6	25	(40)	(55)	35	(30)	BL	BL	5	40	145	BL
S-15						(25)	(25)	(45)	140	(115)	55
A-5	10	20	20	35	(30)	BL	BL	BL	BL	145	BL
A-6	70	35	(45)	55	(30)	5	BL	10	BL	110	BL
A-28						(5)	(10)		110		90

BL indicates the objective was mastered at entry (baseline).

No entry indicates the child was not yet ready for work on the objective.

Parentheses indicate objective was not mastered as of 6/77.

LITERATURE CITED

(For a more extensive bibliography see the Suggested Readings, pages 177–181.)

Creak, M. 1964. Schizophrenic syndrome in childhood. Further progress report of a working party. Dev. Med. Child Neurol. 4:530–535.

Huberty, C. J., Quirk, J. P., and Swan, W. W. 1973. An evaluation system for a psychoeducational treatment program for emotionally disturbed children. Educ. Technol. 13(5):73–82.

Kuglemass, I. 1970. The Autistic Child. Charles C Thomas, Springfield, Ill.

Lotter, V. 1967. Epidemiology of autistic conditions in young children: II. Some characteristics of the parents and children. Soc. Psychiatry 1:163–173.

National Society for Autistic Children. 1973. National Information and Referral Service for Autistic and Autistic-like Persons. National Society for Autistic Children, Inc., Albany, N. Y.

Rimland, B. 1964. Infantile Autism: The Syndrome and Its Implications for a Neutral Theory of Behavior. Appleton-Century-Crofts, Inc., New York.

Ritvo, E. R., Cantwell, D., Johnson, E., Clements, M., Benbrook, F., Slagle, S., Kelly, P., and Ritz, M. 1971. Social class factors in autism. J. Autism Child. Schizo. 1(3):297–310.

Ruttenberg, B., and Wolf, E. 1967. Evaluating the communication of the autistic child. J. Speech Hear. Disord. 32:314–324.

Rutter, M. 1970. The description and classification of infantile autism. Proceedings of the Indiana University colloquium on infantile autism. Charles C Thomas, Springfield, Ill.

Schopler, E. 1965. Early infantile autism and receptor processes. Arch. Gen. Psychiatry 13:327–335.

Schopler, E., and Reichler, R. J. 1971. Parents as cotherapists in the treatment of psychotic children. J. Autism Child. Schizo. 1:87–102.

Swan, W. W. 1971. The development of an observational instrument based on the objectives of developmental therapy. Unpublished doctoral dissertation. University of Georgia, College of Education.

Swan, W. W., and Wood, M. M. 1975. Making decisions about treatment effectiveness. *In* M. M. Wood (ed.), Developmental Therapy, pp. 37–59. University Park Press, Baltimore.

Treffert, D. A. 1970. Epidemiology of infantile autism. Arch. Gen. Psychiatry 22:431–438.

Wing, L. 1974. Children Apart, Autistic Children and Their Families. National Society for Autistic Children, Inc. Albany, N. Y.

Wood, M. M. (ed.). 1972. The Rutland Center Model for Treating Emotionally Disturbed Children. Eric No. ED 087703. Rutland Center Technical Assistance Office, Athens, Ga.

part 2
THE STAGE ONE CLASS:
TWO HOURS OF INTENSITY

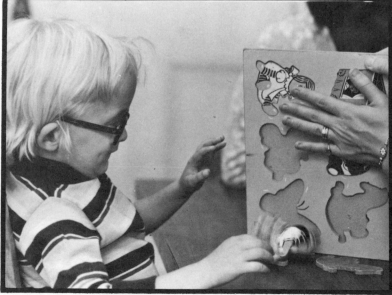

Can you imagine being with four or five extremely disorganized, self-stimulating, or impulsive children who are perhaps hyperactive or who seem barely able to move? Can you imagine attempting to notice their every action, listening for every noise they make, and responding precisely as needed in a therapeutic way? That is what this curriculum is all about.

You must absorb everything that happens and respond constantly. Warmth and consistency are essential. Often you forget your own identity and draw only on those parts of yourself that are therapeutic (helpful and growth-producing). Fatigue, anger, resentment, or detachment are put aside during class time in order to give each child what he needs. What all CSID children require is a pleasurable environment. It is your job to see that every activity produces *responses from every child that result in pleasure*. The difficult part is that each child will have a unique way of experiencing pleasure. This is one of the challenges of teaching Stage One CSID children.

These children's problems are enormous: severe language deficits, perhaps no language (speech) at all, extreme disorganization, strange responses to materials, nonconstructive body motions, sometimes no feeding or toileting skills, and often a mystifying inability to relate to people. With four or five such children in a group, one wonders where to begin!

First, consider the developmental needs of each child. This is done by using the Developmental Therapy Objectives Rating Form (DTORF). This gives you an assessment of the child's current level of functioning in Behavior, Communication, Socialization and (Pre)Academics. It also provides you with educational objectives, which are required under P.L. 94-142 as a part of each child's individualized education program (IEP).

Next, prepare a compilation of the DTORFs for every child in the group. This gives you a group DTORF showing which developmental objectives all of the children are working on and which objectives are needed by only a few of the children. The group DTORF is very important as you begin planning the schedule, activities, and materials you will use.

THE SCHEDULE

The next step is to outline the general sequence of activities that you will conduct in the same order each day. A typical schedule might look like this:

1. Play Time[1]
2. Hello Time
3. Work Time[1]
4. Exercise Time
5. Yum-Yum Time (Tasting and Smelling)
6. Story Time
7. Dance Time (Movement)
8. Outside Time
9. Snack Time[1]
10. Bathroom Time
11. Sand or Water Time
12. Art Time
13. Music Time[1]
14. Good-bye Time

While the name of the activity, its location in the room, and the general concept remain the same throughout the treatment period, the specific materials and activities may vary from week to week or from day to day as the children's interests and skills change. Very often with CSID Stage One children activities may remain practically unchanged, because these children need much time to become comfortable and willing to risk a response.

Vary the location of each activity so the children do not have to sit or stay in one area for more than one activity at a time. This simple change helps keep the children aroused, involves different muscle groups and learning modalities, and helps the children learn that different responses are used in each

---

[1]These activities represent a basic core that we recommend for inclusion in every schedule. This way a teacher can be sure of having experiences in each of the four curriculum areas—Behavior, Communication, Socialization, and (Pre)Academics. It has been our experience that creative activities are vital to the development of Stage One children. Music Time is included here as one of the basic core activities. However, other creative activities such as Art Time, Dance Time, and Story Time can be substituted for Music Time. Ideally all four activities should be included in each two-hour session. For examples of these four creative activities and the other activities listed here, see the learning experiences contained in Part 5 of this text.

activity. For example, activities might involve sitting at the table for Work Time, moving to the floor for Exercise Time, going to the sand table for Sand Time ... to the floor for Story Time, and then ... table for Snack Time.

... strates a floor plan of a Stage One ... provide several such activity areas. ... er to the activity list above and ... o the type of activity conducted in ... more than one activity occurs in the ... the activities usually should not immediately follow each other. You will notice that an exception occurs with activities 2 (Hello Time) and 3 (Work Time). We have found this sequence works if Hello Time is brief and arousing and Work Time is motivating. If you seem to have difficulty sustaining each child's attention during Work Time, you might try moving Hello Time to the floor area. Then the children will have a change of setting for Work Time.

Simple, predictable, consistent routine is all-important in putting together the Stage One experience for CSID children. In a daily, two-hour treatment period, about 12 to 14 activities should be planned. These activities may last only minutes for the first week or two. Gradually, as the children's attention spans increase, the activities may be lengthened. Once the routine is established, it should be faithfully repeated each day. This means that even if time is running out every activity is included, although some activities may be considerably shortened. We feel this careful repetition builds security and trust in the children toward the adults and toward the program itself. The children know what to expect, and they know it will be pleasurable.

Each activity has the same intrinsic organization; this is helpful for the children in learning to respond and for the teacher in conducting the activity. We find it helpful to think of the organization of every activity in six steps.

1. Announcing the Activity

The teacher announces the beginning of an activity after a previous activity is completed, "*Play time is over. Now it's work time.*" The teacher says this while kneeling or stooping down so that she is in each child's line of vision. This is verbalized with much enthusiasm, many smiles, and much touching. After all, the routine is established not for the teacher's convenience but for the child's benefit and pleasure. This must be conveyed to the children.

2. Making the Transition

The teacher verbalizes, again warmly and happily, and signs (if signing is being used in the class), "*Sit in chair.*" The teacher moves to the table, leading the most willing, organized children with her. The support teacher brings up the stragglers and reorganizes them by verbalizing again, "*Sit in chair.*" The children are touched or gently led, if necessary, until everyone is sitting in his chair. Sometimes the teacher may show the next activity's materials during the transition to arouse the attention of a child who does not want to come to the activity or who is becoming disorganized.[2]

3. Renaming the Activity

The teacher verbalizes (signs, too) the name of the activity again, "*It's work time!*" She may attempt to have particular children repeat the word "*work.*" A few children with high Stage One communication objectives may be encouraged to respond, without a response model, to the question, "*What comes next?*"

The lead teacher tries to get each child to attend to her and to what she is saying. She may repeat her announcement several times, directing the verbalization to each child individually and pairing words with a touch to help the child become aware of the teacher.

4. Conducting the Activity

Now the teacher quickly pulls out her materials (which have been concealed but which are also easily available) and dramatically and enthusiastically pursues the activity that she has very carefully planned. During *each* activity the teacher must interact with every child *at least* once a minute.

Rating each child on the Developmental Therapy objectives gives a clear view of what should

---

[2]As noted previously, not all activities are conducted at the table with the children sitting in chairs. However, this example of a transition can be followed as an effective format in moving the group to any area of the room or to sit on the floor.

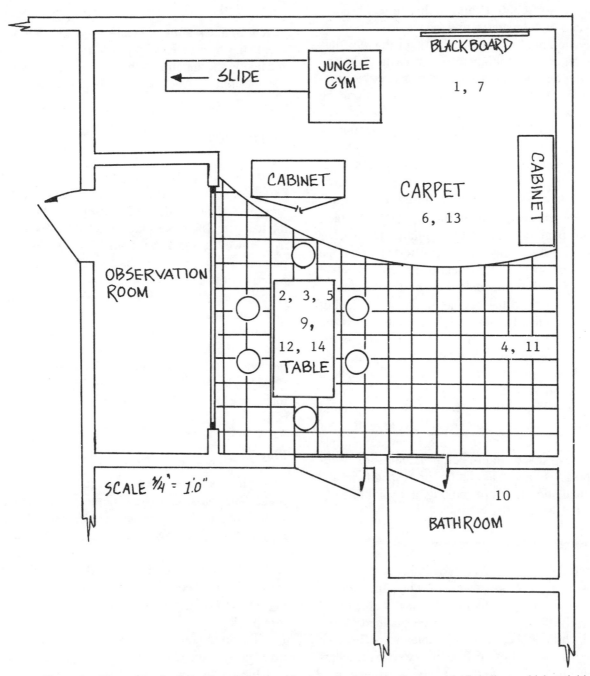

Figure 1. Floor plan of a Stage One classroom. Numbers, keyed to the list on page 17, indicate which activities are performed in each area. (Drawn by Maggie Andrews.)

be emphasized during each activity. Then the activity can be sequenced into the following steps:

a. Arousal: It is necessary to arouse the nonattending, out-of-contact child so that he will become aware of the material and the teacher. This may be attempted with voice, body, or the materials at hand. By getting to know each child and trying various approaches, the teacher becomes aware of the unique way each child can be aroused.

b. Attention: The next step is getting attention or focus. That is, the child must be encouraged to look at either the teacher herself or at a material such as a bright piece of construction paper.

c. Response: For each child the teacher has different expectations for the response. In fact, with beginning Stage One children the teacher may have to concentrate her efforts only on the first or second step mentioned. Any positive move toward the materials or the teacher is accepted from the beginning Stage One child. He may merely look at the material, may reach for it, or may explore it in some way. As the child progresses, responses can be taught, even if the child is unwilling or unable to make a response spontaneously.

d. Result: Every response requested of a child should result in a good or satisfying feeling for him. Of course, these feelings can be as simple as low-keyed, nonspecific feelings of well-being, as intense as elation, or as specific as the visual stimulation of looking at a sparkling object.

5. Closing

By carefully and sensitively watching the group, the teacher soon becomes aware of when the activity needs to end. Very often a teacher is not able to get completely through what has been planned before several children begin to lose interest or become diverted to other stimuli. Experience helps teachers learn whether to pursue the activity as planned or to cut it short. When a teacher's priority is enjoyment and success for the children, she soon learns this timing.

When she feels it is time to begin concluding an activity, the teacher announces, *"Work time is almost over."* Although these words are usually mean-

ingless at first for the children, they soon learn that the activity will be ending shortly.

6. Ending

A few minutes after the "almost over" announcement, the teacher says, *"Work time is over."* Immediately she announces the next activity, *"Now it's _____ time."* And the cycle begins again.

ACTIVITIES

While each Stage One class will be designed with a variety of activities suited to the needs of that particular group, it should also reflect the particular skills of the teacher. There is room for considerable creativity. However, we have found four activities that provide a core for a well balanced program. These four activities are play, work, snack, and a creative experience (art, story, music, or movement). By including these four activities, you can be assured of opportunities to work on the objectives in all four areas of the Developmental Therapy curriculum—Behavior, Communication, Socialization, and (Pre)Academics. Because of their importance, these four basic activities are described in some detail below.

Play Time

Play Time is a good way to begin the day. In our Stage One classroom, half of the floor is covered with "hot pink" shag carpet. The carpet defines the play area by appealing to the children's sense of sight and touch. Cardboard blocks, a small jungle gym with a slide on one side, and a cabinet stocked with toys—all have been carefully chosen to be stimulating and arousing for the particular children in the group.

Having Play Time at the beginning of the class gives most Stage One children a chance to get comfortable in the room and to move whatever interests them in the play area. There is often tremendous variability in a CSID child's behavior, a characteristic which is quite obvious in his attempts to play. Play Time provides you with a chance to observe very carefully the way each child may be functioning on that particular day.

Play Time is generally a less structured activity than most of the other activities. The child has freedom to move around the play area and to respond (or perhaps not respond) to whatever he wants. Observing the children during this time gives you much important information about the level at which each child is functioning and can help you to experiment with new ways to interact and make psychological contact with each child.

Even though it is less structured than other activities, it is important to keep in contact verbally and often physically with every child at least once each minute of the play activity. This feat can be especially difficult because the children probably are doing different things and are scattered all over the play area. Thus, team work with other teachers or parents in the room is essential during play.

Each contact you make should be both verbal and physical. Reflect what the child is doing, *"Mike has blocks,"* or perhaps just say *"blocks"* and provide a gentle touch. These simple, reflective statements and physical contacts convey information to the child about what he is doing. They also tell him that you think his efforts, even though they may be minimal, are important.

Especially in the beginning weeks it is not necessary to work for qualitative responses to the activities and materials. During Play Time find ways to give each child pleasurable experiences at his own level. One child came into the Stage One class with negative, resistant, disorganized behavior. He did not want to do anything and would not participate. The one thing he did enjoy doing was picking up two small blocks and throwing them a few feet away, crawling after them, then throwing them again. Every attempt to show the child some exciting, simple play material was ignored or met with screams. Then one day his teacher joined him. She began to play the throw and fetch game alongside him, then with him. The teacher showed acceptance and pleasure at what the child was doing and soon established a beginning relationship, creatively built from the child's perseverative, disorganized world.

Play Time is a good opportunity to experiment with different forms of physical contact that might be both pleasurable and arousing for each child. It also provides opportunities to work on objectives in each of the four curriculum areas—Behavior, Communication, Socialization, and (Pre)Academics. During Play Time you often may be the only model for how to play. Involve yourself enthusiastically with the play materials. In this way you can begin to gradually involve a child in responding to them. Consider a child who is standing, staring at the wall. You could approach him, carrying several cardboard blocks. Once in his field of vision, begin stacking the blocks noisily, saying gleefully, *"Blocks! Look! I have blocks."* After the blocks are stacked, knock them down. Show much excitement and pleasure. Quickly begin stacking again, verbally reflecting the activity. It may be a long time before the child's response is more than attending. Perhaps you might try handing a block to him, gesturing what to do, or letting him touch the block as you complete the process. By gradually involving the child with the materials, you can teach the child to stack the blocks or to play with other materials. This block procedure may not work the first time, maybe not the second time, but if you see any response or awareness, continue encouraging, luring him to participate. Gradually you can expect him to do it himself.

Some CSID children at Stage One do not profit from the relative freedom of movement and choice during Play Time. The very nonresponsive child as well as the extremely impulsive, disorganized child are two examples. The nonresponsive child who perceives little of his environment needs much physical intervention and exposure to many arousing materials before he becomes aware of the play experience. You will need to attempt constantly to make contact with the child through your body, face, voice, and the sensory materials in the play area. Soft furry balls, bright shiny rings, an old clock that ticks and rings, and a big wooden truck to ride are some materials that have worked for us. Try to arouse the child with a great variety of materials and demonstrate a simple response that he could model. In contrast, the restless, disorganized child may be responding to all of the stimuli in the room without selectively screening out stimuli from those that warrant a response. Or the child may be engaged in self-stimulating activities, active but oblivious to what is around him. Like the nonresponding child, this child also needs structure and assistance in order to focus on particular materials and to learn a satisfying response.

Play Time always involves clean-up activities. All children are involved in clean-up, even when some have to be moved through the process. Likewise, all children receive praise for helping to clean up.

There is an activity in Part 5 describing how clean-up can be achieved while also working on other objectives during Play Time.

Work Time

We call this activity "Table Time" because we want the children to associate the activities with table tasks. Work Time provides an optimal opportunity for working with each child on his own objectives. Every child may have a different task; however, if two or more children are able to work on the same task, plan for them to work at the same time. During Work Time you have the opportunity to plan specific tasks to enhance the strengths and to minimize the deficits of each child. Encourage tasks that involve fine motor and perceptual skills such as working with paper, crayons, or felt tip markers, stringing beads, and stacking blocks or rings.

In the beginning when children are new to the routine, probably uncomfortable at sitting, and possessors of short attention spans, Work Time might include only one activity for each child and may last only a few minutes. However, as the children become more comfortable with sitting and working, Work Time may include two or three activities lasting about 10 minutes (for example, learning to scribble with crayon and paper, then stacking blocks, and then stringing beads). This activity and its length depend entirely on the children's skills and the skills of the teachers at helping each child learn to accomplish the task with a resulting feeling of pleasure.

Language should be a focus in every activity with CSID children. Of course, the type of language expectation will depend on the child's developmental objectives. As this activity begins, you have an opportunity to *label* the materials each child has. (For example, show a child blocks and say, "*Mike has blocks!*" Then hand the blocks to Mike). First, you work for *awareness* from the child. Then, perhaps after a few days or weeks, suspend the material directly in front of the child, hoping for a spontaneous response to it. As a child's awareness and understanding increase, you can begin to expect more from him. The child can be expected to produce a sound in order to receive the material. Then, perhaps, an approximation of the word may be expected; in time, a word will emerge. You can see how critical it is for the material (or task) to be something that the child really likes. In addition, it is necessary to balance repetition of familiar materials with the introduction of new ones.

Because each Stage One child needs constant intervention to stay at his task during Work Time, it is usually necessary to have several adults working with the children. It is their responsibility to keep the children working successfully. However, if a child does not need constant intervention, one teacher can lead the Work Time, assisting individual children as needed with the help of a support teacher. Whatever arrangement you work out, you should be sure to make some contact with every child intermittently during the activity. Another good time to provide contact with simple words and appropriate physical contact is at the completion of the activity.

Satisfactory accomplishment of the tasks is the goal. Activities must be devised for each child that can bring this satisfaction. When the task is difficult for a child, intervene and assist him to a successful outcome. You will notice that as the child's skills for a specific task increase, the need for your physical intervention will decrease.

Snack Time

This activity is often called "Juice and Cookies Time" or "Milk and Cookies Time." It is an excellent opportunity to elicit language and work on socialization objectives. Having Snack Time follow an outside activity or midway in the day's activities will be rewarding because the children will be thirsty and usually eager for something refreshing.

From the very beginning be aware of each child's likes and dislikes: whether he likes white or chocolate milk, which type of juice he favors, and which cookies he likes. It may be necessary to have several types of juice and cookies to satisfy each child. Whatever you provide, it *must be* desirable to a child in order to elicit beginning sounds or word approximations. Once the child's preferences are established, you are able to push for beginning communication.

Each child is expected to indicate that he wants juice and cookies, but the way that each child asks will be an individual matter. It is important that this expectation is conveyed in a very positive manner. The message is: You can use words (sounds) to get what you want.

If a child is able to make a consistent sound, give him juice only when he produces this sound.[3] Also, give a very small amount at each request so that he will request again. It is likely that if you provide a half-filled cup of juice on the first request it may be a sufficient amount and the child will have no further need to request juice. Therefore, give only a small amount at a time. Do the same with cookies; provide only a small piece for each request. The important expectation in Snack Time is communication and arbitrarily limiting the number of cookies seems counter-productive to this purpose. The guideline that has worked best for us is to make cookies (small pieces) available as long as 1) the child is requesting the cookies and 2) the attention of the group is high for the activity.

For children who have not yet acquired definite sound patterns, determine whether a look at you or a gesture toward the juice would be acceptable. Whatever criterion you establish for obtaining juice, follow the response with exaggerated sound patterns while giving the child the juice. Have the child touch your lips with his fingers. Insist that any children who can say the whole word *"juice"* do so. Then, very gradually, encourage and only accept a sequence of words such as, *"I want juice."* Because Snack Time usually is refreshing and rewarding for children, it is an excellent time to expand the use of word sequence with children who have higher skills. It is also a good time to encourage talking with another child or sharing with another child.

Children sometimes become frustrated or angry when you withhold juice or cookies for language. They might even have tantrums. Manage this by

---

[3]The success of these procedures will depend primarily upon the gentle, supportive tone you convey.

reflecting, *"It makes you mad to say juice. You can say juice."* Be sure the child receives immediate praise for making the appropriate response (for example, by reflecting, *"Good! Maria said juice"*). Then immediately give the child the juice. It is important, also, to build up expectations *gradually*.

Toward the end of Snack Time, always announce that this activity is *"Almost over,"* giving each child an opportunity to obtain more juice and cookies before the activity ends.

Music Time

Music Time can be the most rewarding activity of the day if you can find the type of music activity that arouses and brings pleasure to each child in the group. If not, you will find that music will terrify some CSID children. Rhythm band instruments are especially useful. Choose instruments that are luring with stimulating sounds or soft songs that are calming and soothing. The loudness or large size of some instruments can be frightening to a child. Therefore, it is important to watch each child's reactions to the instruments. If a child pulls back, begins self-stimulation, or cries, gently move him so that he touches the instrument. Cuddle or gently pat the child. Physically reassure him that it is all right and that no harm will come to him. Help him to have a pleasurable experience from his contact with the instrument.

Many music activities lend themselves easily to learning imitation skills. This is particularly important for CSID children beginning Stage One. A drum or shaker is especially easy to use. Simple action songs are good for more advanced Stage One children, and marching and action songs involving gross motor movements are good with nearly all children.

It is important to keep each child involved in every activity. You may have to begin by moving a child through the motions involved in playing an instrument. When you feel he has the motion, pull back and let him go on his own. If the child stops when you pull back, move in again until he learns the motion on his own. One thing for which you will especially need to watch is allowing enough opportunity for a child to do as much as possible independently. Remember, also, that this may take *much, much* longer than for nonhandicapped children.

Always give the child the name for each instrument and verbalize what you are doing as you demonstrate: "*Hit the drum,*" "*Strum the guitar,*" or "*Shake the shakers,*" etc.

When giving the child a new instrument, always give him an opportunity to explore it. Help him feel different parts of it carefully, reinforcing the pleasurable response to the sensory experience. If one child is strumming the guitar and another child comes over to play it, encourage the second child to pat the side of the guitar while the other child is playing.

Once the children are comfortable with the instruments and want to use them, begin to work on Communication objectives by soliciting speech sounds to obtain an instrument.

For higher developmental levels, you can encourage parallel play on some instruments, sound patterns, or sing-a-long in songs. Sometimes the request may be simply to fill in one or two words or the sound of an animal (as with "Old MacDonald Had a Farm").

TECHNIQUES

Being able to relate to a child in a predictable, consistent manner is the beginning of building trust. You must work hard at learning how to make psychological contact with each child; however, this may take weeks. One child may show pleasure from having his hand held, another from having his hair tousled, another from having his back stroked, another from having his own jargon repeated back to him, and another from brushing his hand across your face or hair. *With beginning Stage One children the first priority is to arouse the child's attention level and to give him pleasure from that arousal.* In doing this, be sensitive, also, to the possibility that your attempts at arousal may be frightening, confusing, or too intrusive. There is a fine line between finding a way to arouse a child and maintaining respect for the child's personal boundaries. If the arousal gives him pleasure, you have found a means to increase his ability to stay in touch with his environment.

Finding what is both arousing and pleasurable for each child is a difficult task. A child's specific sensory strengths and deficits may not yet be evident because testing a CSID child is difficult and very little may be known when he arrives in your class. This means you must observe the child carefully for clues as to what both arouses and gives pleasure. Often the self-stimulatory behaviors in which a child is already engaging may give you clues. For instance, if a child rocks himself spontaneously, try rocking the child yourself, using your body as a means of arousing as well as giving pleasure. Then, it would be important in such an activity to introduce some new dimensions, perhaps awareness of you. Otherwise the child may further lose awareness of his environment. This may mean rocking a child so that he is facing you, singing his name softly, or making eye contact. It is possible that such activities may fail to give much arousal or awareness, but in time they could lead to a rocking or swinging game that the child eventually expects.

Learning to relate to a nonresponding child is like learning to relate to a new infant, except it is far more difficult. Nevertheless, the attempts people make to lure an infant into looking and responding, such as "peek-a-boo," cooing, and laughing, are similar to what must be done to relate to a severely impaired CSID child. Your usual repertoire of behaviors and your own particular voice quality or personality may need to be expanded and polished to get the results you want from a particular child. Animation in voice, face, and body are proven attention getters for these children. However, what arouses one child may frighten another. You must be sensitive and flexible.

Once you have found several ways to help a child respond, there are five specific techniques that can be used in almost any activity to assist him in expanding his awareness of the environment.

Controlled Vocabulary

Because many Stage One children usually have severe difficulties not only with speaking but also with understanding what is said, it is important to carefully select and control the amount of language you will use in the classroom and at home. By carefully selecting and repeating simple language patterns, you can begin to help each child label and give meaning to his routine and the materials he uses. Functional, concrete words, both nouns and verbs, give a relevance to the communication act which is essential if you want to provide a child with *reasons* to speak.

Between teachers and parents there must be absolute consistency in the words used to communicate to the children. It is important, also, to remain consistent with word order and tense as much as possible. Sometimes writing down specific words and phrases and posting them inconspicuously on the wall is helpful in the classroom and at home. This specification and control of the language used by adults is referred to as "controlled vocabulary." It may be compared with the language patterns a mother instinctively uses when trying to communicate with a one-year-old baby.

The "controlled vocabulary" we use with Stage One children who have no speech usually is a limited number of words selected to have direct reference to home and classroom activities and materials (e.g., "milk," "cookies," "paste," "work time," "play time," etc.) The child, hearing simple, consistent language patterns with a clear relationship to something tangible, has only a few models to imitate at first. Because some CSID children are confused and have no functional speech, limiting the variety of inputs is essential to progress in the beginning. It is equally important to use the selected words in as many situations as possible.

Reflecting Statements

Reflecting statements require no response from a child. Labeling the materials and routine of the room are typical reflecting statements. Examples are: *"It's work time." "Truck, tr-uck." "Work time is over." "Maria is pasting." "Maria sees the bubbles." "Paper, pa-per." "Maria touched Mike." "Milk, m-ilk." "I have milk."* It may be necessary to have your face very close to a child or to touch him to enable him to connect your sounds with his activity. Or, you might try banging on the paper with your hand to emphasize the syllables in the word, *"paper."* Always combine these simple verbalizations with gentle touching of the child. Perhaps just get-

ting down close to his face will help him know you are talking. Generally, reflections directed to the group go unheeded. You may have to repeat them individually to each child.

Commands

Because commands require specific behavioral responses, they cannot be used effectively until a child has mastered at least the first two objectives in Behavior (B-0 and B-1). (Refer to the Appendix.) Some examples of commands include: *"Sit in the chair." "Play time is on the rug." "Mike, pick up the coat." "Toys go in the cabinet." "Put in." "Stand up." "Let's go outside." "Run." "Drink juice." "Give me the puzzle."* Commands are said with the expectation that the child will give some motor response. Commands must convey the expectation of the motor response. To teach this, it is often helpful to begin by pairing commands with physical intervention (for example, "motoring" a child through the expected responses; see Physical Intervention below).

Echoing

This is a technique for encouraging a child's babbling and jargon by repeating his sounds back to him. This echoing is done most frequently after a child babbles or when no sounds are being made during activities. Echoing should not be used during times when normal verbalizations are needed for instructions, introduction of activities, verbal encouragement, etc.

Be sensitive as to what specific sounds each child in the class makes. For instance, one child may say *"Na-na-na"* and *"Oi-oi-oi."* When you learn the sounds that each child makes, you can repeat them to the child as a method of relating to him as well as encouraging these sounds. This leads to imitation of other simple babbling sounds which you can introduce later. However, if you make these sounds in response to a child's babbling and he stops every time you do this, it should be a clue that this procedure is not pleasurable to the child and it is better to stop using it. Although this technique is primarily a verbal/auditory method, a child must also have visual cues. When you repeat sounds, be sure you are within the child's view so that he can see how your articulators (teeth, lips, and tongue) form the sounds. Encourage the child to touch your mouth while you make the sounds, especially for the plosives (*t, p, k, b, ch, sh*), which emit air from the mouth. This gives the child the tactile cues that can also aid in teaching him formation of sounds.

Physical Intervention

"Moving a child through it" is the way we describe a teacher physically moving the child's hand or body to complete a task. Others call it "motoring." This moving is done gently but with sureness on your part. For example, if a child is directed to "*pick up*" but avoids or does not respond, put your hand on the top of his hand and assist him in picking up the object and placing it appropriately. In this way the child learns what "pick up" means. Gradually, as the child gains awareness and willingness to follow the direction, pull back physically, allowing him to complete more and more of the task on his own. If you are not careful to pull back, the child may become dependent on you to move him each time.

Sometimes teachers and parents are confused by the terms *touch, physical intervention,* and *redirection. Touch* is used to psychologically reach a child, reminding him of your presence and perhaps arousing him. Touch does no more than this. In contrast, *physical intervention* provides the child with assistance in making the expected motor response. It is important that physical intervention always be accomplished with a gentle, supportive quality even in times of crisis. *Redirection* is used to assist a child when his responses are becoming disorganized. He is provided with whatever type of remotivation and support he needs to continue. This may involve both controlled vocabulary and physical intervention. *Successful use of each of these techniques results in a child's return to an activity in which he continues to participate with pleasure.*

part 3
SAMPLE
HOME PROGRAMS

It is essential that assistance in home management be provided to parents of CSID children. Because the situation within each family has its own unique characteristics, every family's home program will be different. We have found that collaborative planning with parents is the best way to develop the home program. Parents are in the best position to select the specific objectives because they know what the urgent problems are and where the greatest family stress occurs. Parents also will be able to provide information about the materials and activities their child enjoys and those he fears.

We often start planning with parents by finding ways to have a more structured home routine. We try to determine the times a child is particularly disorganized or disruptive and to plan a specific activity or experience that focuses clearly upon this problem. Family activities that often cause the greatest stress include mealtime, toileting, bedtime, and leisure. Sometimes it is feasible to begin a home program that focuses on only one activity. In other instances, parents feel that every home routine should have a plan.

After parents have had success in implementing a home program aimed at establishing fairly comfortable management of daily home routines, they often want to expand the home program to include visits to the grocery store and the public playground. When these trips go smoothly, the possibilities for socializing a CSID child expand immensely.

After the specific family activity(ies) is selected, the next step is to identify specific objectives that will be the program focus. These objectives also should help the parents determine when procedures have been successful and when it is time to change the home program objectives and procedures. We have found that it is best to limit the first program to a few Developmental Therapy objectives. Preferably the parents make the selection from their child's baseline Developmental Therapy Objective Rating Form (DTORF).

Once the objectives have been chosen, work together with the parents to get the program going. Sometimes it helps to have the parents observe you in the classroom demonstrating the techniques and activities to be used at home. In other instances it is better to demonstrate the program in the child's home. This seems to be helpful to parents who have had considerable difficulty in establishing home routines. Other parents are able to put the home program into action without a teacher's demonstration. In any case, it is essential to plan to visit the home *at least* once every week until the program is clearly in operation and the parents have had evident success. During the early phases of a home program it may be necessary to visit several times a week.

However often you plan to visit, be sure that a mutually satisfactory schedule is arranged with the parents. They should know that they can expect you at a very specific time, on specific days, and for a specific length of time. It is important to keep to this schedule. Looseness in keeping the schedule works against efforts to establish a consistent, predictable family routine and often jeopardizes the relationship between the parents and teacher.

Each home program should be written in a style useful to a particular family. Parents should be given a written program but the amount of record keeping requested of the parent will vary. Some parents feel that keeping daily charts of activities and accomplishments helps them to keep up with the program; often small increments of progress can be noted in such daily records. In contrast, other parents respond to the idea of record keeping as an impossible burden; in these situations it is better to encourage the parents to direct their energies into actually conducting the program, becoming keen observers who can communicate effectively with you about their children's progress.

We have selected five home programs to illustrate the range of program styles and formats that we have used. In each example, the child's name is fictitious.

SALLY'S HOME PROGRAM

Sally is a CSID, cerebral palsied, nonambulatory, four-year-old child who functions below the level of a nonhandicapped four-month-old infant. Her manual skills were minimal, but she showed a slight preference for the right hand. Her greatest asset was frequent eye following with occasional direct eye contact. The following is a home program planned by the CSID staff with the help of Sally's mother. Because of transportation difficulties, Sally was unable to attend the daily Stage One class, but her mother was willing to implement this program at home each day. Twice each week Sally was brought to the center by her family for follow-up and teacher-parent teamwork.

On the first few visits Sally's mother observed the teacher working with Sally through the one-way mirror. After two sessions, the mother came into the room with the teacher, and together they conducted the activities and shared information about the child's functioning and responses. The teacher prepared Sally's mother for beginning the program at home. The following week Sally's mother conducted the activities at the center with the teacher giving suggestions and support.

Currently Sally's mother is doing this home program on a daily basis. They continue to come to the center twice a week. The parent and teacher take turns doing the therapy session and exchange ideas, suggestions for new activities, and expectations.

DEVELOPMENTAL THERAPY OBJECTIVES (DTORF)

Behavior

B-1: to react to sensory stimulus by attending toward source of stimulus by body response or by looking (in situations using tactile, motor, visual, auditory, tasting, or smell stimuli)

B-2: to respond to stimulus by sustained attending toward source of stimulus (continued looking at object or person after initial stimulus-response has occurred)

B-3: to respond spontaneously to simple environmental stimulus with a motor behavior: object, person, sound

Communication

C-0: to produce sounds

C-1: to attend to person speaking (Child moves or looks toward adult when adult initiates verbal stimulus. Eye contact not necessary.)

C-2: to respond to verbal stimulus with a motor behavior (Object present; teacher does not use gestures.)

Socialization

S-1: to be aware of others (Child looks at adult or another child when adult or another child speaks directly to child or touches him.)

S-2: to attend to other's behavior (Child looks at another when attention is not on child directly.)

S-3: to respond to adult when child's name is called (Child looks at adult or away; appropriate or inappropriate response acceptable.)

The home program given to Sally's mother appears on page 31.

SALLY'S SCHEDULE FOR JANUARY

Try to do each of these activities at least once every day.

1. Play Time: Use various objects that make a sound or feel interesting, such as an old wind-up clock, a radio, or cow bells. Help her to explore the objects with her hands. Try to keep them in her field of vision.

   Touch her body with yours. Pull her arms and rock with her. Exercise her arms and hands. Massage her body.

   Use your imagination to think of different materials, different activities, anything that might interest her and give her pleasure.

2. Fingerpaint: Use a large piece of paper and move her hands through the paint. Gradually release your grasp and let her move her hands on her own in the material (shaving cream, whipped cream, sour cream, or yogurt are good substitutes).

3. Water Play: After painting, have her walk to the sink to rinse her hands. Put her on a box if necessary so she can reach the water. Make the water an activity. Soap her up to her elbows; make it fun; encourage her to splash and play.

4. Juice and Cookies: Have her walk back to the table. Use a long cookie (better for grasping). This is the time to get her to make sounds. See that she gives you some sound for every bit and sip of juice (or milk) even if she gets mad! Continue to talk to her, smiling and laughing all the time. Help her enjoy the experience.

5. Blocks: Dump out the three blocks from the form box. Help her to get all three blocks back in! Remember to keep her left hand out of the way.

Encourage Sally to:

Look at you and objects.
Hold objects (especially in her right hand).
Touch different textures: water, sand, the rug, the floor, your face, your hair, her own body, the grass, anything and everything. You help her do it!

Encourage her sisters to:

Smile and talk to her to teach her to enjoy doing things and being with people.
Touch her and caress her when they talk to her. Let her know they are there.
Either hold her left hand or occupy it in some way. Get the right hand to work!

Keep up the good work!

JOHN'S HOME PROGRAM

The following is a home program designed entirely around music activities for a three-and-a-half-year-old CSID boy. The main purpose of this program was to help the boy's mother learn to work with him in a structured situation at home so that a better relationship could develop between herself and her son.

Improved relationships at home were needed if he was to continue to make any progress. John's mother was given the written program which follows without the objectives, and she was given a cassette tape on which all the songs for the program were pretaped to help her learn them. This program also included a form for recording the time spent each day on each activity. Because the purpose of this program was to initiate pleasurable moments between mother and son, more extensive recording was thought to be counter-productive at this point.

The music therapist, the parent worker, and the mother worked together once a week at the center with John. They discussed activities and techniques and evaluated the effectiveness of each activity. Each week the program was modified as John progressed.

DEVELOPMENTAL THERAPY OBJECTIVES (DTORF)

Behavior

B-2: to respond to stimulus by sustained attending toward source of stimulus (continued looking at object or person after initial stimulus-response has occurred)

B-3: to respond spontaneously to simple environmental stimulus with a motor behavior: object, person, sound

B-4: to respond with motor and body responses to complex environmental and verbal stimuli (through imitation "Do this;" through completion of verbal direction; or through minimal participation in activities) given physical intervention and verbal cues

Communication

C-2: to respond to verbal stimulus with a motor behavior (Object present; teacher does not use gestures.)

C-3: to respond to verbal stimulus and single object with a recognizable approximation of the appropriate verbal response (Child gives verbal approximation to indicate use or correct answer to question, "What is this?" Object present; function or name acceptable.)

Socialization

S-4: child interacts with adult nonverbally to meet needs

S-5: to engage in organized solitary play (with direction from adult if necessary; age-appropriate play not necessary)

S-6: to respond to adult's verbal and nonverbal requests to come to him (Child moves next to adult and looks at him, and child accepts adult's touch.)

S-7: to demonstrate understanding of single verbal requests or directions given directly to child (Adult does not use gestures.)

(Pre)Academics

A-5: to respond with rudimentary fine and gross motor skills to simple manipulative tasks associated with 24-month age level

The home program given to John's mother appears on pages 33–34.

JOHN'S MUSIC PROGRAM

Activity One

Materials: drum

Steps:

1. Sit facing John.
2. Put the drum between you and John. Say, *"drum."*
3. Hit the drum a few times.
4. Say, *"John, play drum."*
5. If he doesn't begin playing by himself within about 10 seconds, repeat, *"John, play drum."* Help him do it.
6. Both you and John play the drum while you sing the song below. The tune is the same as "Skip to my Lou."

   John and Mommy are playing the drum,
   John and Mommy are playing the drum,
   John and Mommy are playing the drum,
   John and Mommy play the drum.

7. Give him a hug and say, *"Good! John played drum."*

Activity Two

Materials: jingle bells (2)
Steps:

1. When you get his eye on a bell, hold one of the bells below your mouth and say, *"bells."*
2. Give John the bells saying, *"Take bells."*
3. Say, *"John, play bells,"* and show him how.
4. If he doesn't play by himself, help him.
5. Both of you play the bells as you sing the song below. The tune is the same as "Here We Go 'Round the Mulberry Bush."

This is the way we play the bells,
Play the bells,
Play the bells,
This is the way we play the bells,
Play the bells.

6. Say, *"Good playing bells, John."* Touch him or hug him. Smile at him.
7. Say, *"Give me bells."*
8. Hug him and say, *"Bells are gone."*

Activity Three

Materials: None

Steps:

1. Tell John, *"Stand up."* Stand beside him.
2. Sing the song below as you and John walk around in a circular motion. *"Walk with me, walk with me, walk with me, walk with me."*
3. Help John hop around the circle as you sing the second verse. *"Hop with me, hop with me, hop with me, hop with me."*
4. Help John run around the circle as you sing the third verse. *"Run with me, run with me, run with me, run with me."*
5. Sit down and gesture John to sit down as you sing. *"Sit with me, sit with me, sit with me, sit with me."*
6. Praise him at the end of each verse: *"Good walking,"* *"Good hopping,"* *"Good running,"* *"Good sitting."* Give him a hug when he sits down.
7. Sit facing John and hold both his hands. Swing his arms and sway with him as you sing,

   John had fun in music, music, music,
   John had fun in music, music today.

JOHN'S MUSIC TIME

Week of _____

Activities	Mon.	Tues.	Wed.	Thurs.	Fri.	Sat.	Sun.
Total time							

Each time you work with John check off the activities you do and put the total time you spent each day in the corresponding blocks. Please bring this record with you each Friday at 3:00 p.m. so we can plan new activities as they are needed. Also, please give us feedback about the activities such as:

1. Are they appropriate for John?
2. Are you comfortable using them?
3. What are some of the changes that you would like to make in the activities?
4. Do you feel they are helping John?
5. Does John enjoy the program?

Comments and/or questions: _____

_____

_____

NEAL'S HOME PROGRAM

Neal, a five-year-old CSID child, seemed to be on the brink of a significant breakthrough into meaningful speech. What was needed was an all-out, coordinated effort at home and at the center. The home program described here was developed because of his mother's willingness to spend considerable time with Neal at home. This intensive, coordinated effort to stimulate language and cognitive processes at home and at the center resulted in the developmental progress we had hoped for—spontaneous, functional speech.

Neal's home program was divided into two parts. The first was a general language stimulation program which his family applied whenever he was at home. This part of the program consisted of general guidelines for stimulating speech in all home activities and routines.

The second part was a specific "Directed Activity" time to be conducted for approximately 15 minutes each day. This part of the home program was designed to provide a fairly direct extension of the center program with the expectations that directing this bombardment of highly structured activities at Neal would provide extended practice and would result in generalization of learning.

This home program also illustrates the use of index cards of activities prepared by the teacher for the family's use at home. We asked the family to keep a file box of these cards. As Neal learned to do an activity successfully, a new activity card was prepared by the teacher and the old card went into the family's file box. From this collection of successful activities, Neal's family was able to vary the activities between new ones and the familiar, old ones. As he progressed, this "Directed Activity" time was increased in duration, and Neal's family became increasingly successful in selecting and designing the activities to be used each day.

DEVELOPMENTAL THERAPY OBJECTIVES (DTORF)

Communication

C-8: to answer a child's and adult's questions or requests with recognizable, meaningful, relevant word(s)

C-11: to use simple word sequences to command or request of another child or adult in ways acceptable to classroom procedures

(Pre)Academics

A-19: to recognize detail in pictures by gesture or word

A-22: to recognize pictures that are the same and ones that are different (Child must understand teacher's directions: "*Find the one that's the same,*" "*Find the one that's different,*" or comparable statement.)

A-24: to perform eye-hand coordination activities at the five-year level (examples: cuts with scissors along lines and draws a recognizable person with body)

A-25:[1] to recognize symbols, numerals, and written words that are the same and ones that are different

A-28:[1] to discriminate concepts of differences in *up, down; under, over; big, little; tall, short; hot, cold; first, last*

The home program given to Neal's mother appears on pages 36–39.

---

[1]These objectives were added three months later after Neal had mastered A-19 and A-22.

NEAL'S GENERAL LANGUAGE STIMULATION PROGRAM: OCTOBER–DECEMBER (C-8, C-11)

1. Require Neal to ask specifically for things—"*I want*" or "*Give me*"—during meals and dressing times or whenever you offer him something he wants and it is convenient for you to do so.

   > Example: Say, "*I have* (name of object)." "*Do you want____?*" Require Neal to say, "*I want_*" (or "*Give me*").

2. When going somewhere or playing outside with Neal, play the "Stop and Go" game. Hold his hand and say, "*Run,*" over and over again as you run together. Then say, "*Stop,*" when you stop. Follow the same sequence using "*walk.*" Alternate "*run*" and "*walk*" with "*stop.*" Neal will probably be able to say the words after doing this several times. Tell him, "*Say it,*" as you start to run or walk.

3. In order to teach Neal to respond correctly to "*Show me _____,*" say the name of something that Neal likes and can point to. Repeat the name two or three times. Then say, "*Show me _____.*" Repeat the sequence if necessary. After Neal can do this successfully, ask him, "*What is that?*" at the end of the sequence. If he does not answer correctly, say the word for him and again ask, "*What is that?*" Always use a positive, warm, supportive tone of voice. Use this sequence first for objects until he has mastered it. Then use it for naming things in pictures or on food labels.

4. Encourage Neal to use different forms of "*I want _____*" when asking for things. When Neal wants an object, use the model "*Give me _____*" or the question, "*What do you want, Neal?*"

JANUARY–MARCH (C-8, C-11)

1. Work on teaching Neal a question-response structure. Ask him simple questions about objects ("*What is this?*") and people ("*Whose turn is it?*"). Tell him the answer if he doesn't respond and then wait for him to repeat the answer. Praise him when he does it.

   > Example: Ask, "*Whose chair is this?*" Require Neal to say, "*This is Mommy's chair.*" Give him the model if necessary.

2. Use "parallel talk" with Neal during the day when interacting with him. Talk through the task with him. Then give him a word phrase to repeat and wait for him to do so.

   > Example: Say, "*Neal is sweeping the floor. Sweep the floor.*"
   > Wait for Neal to say, "*Sweep the floor.*"

3. Continue to provide opportunities for Neal to use pencil, crayons, and scissors at times when you are around to give him some structure. Have him ask for everything. As he finishes a picture, ask "*What's this?*" as you point to things that he has drawn. Praise him.

4. Allow Neal to help cook or prepare something simple. Structure the activity so that he can put in the ingredients and/or stir them. Emphasize the verbs, *put in, pour, stir.*

   > Example: Ask Neal, "*Do you want flour?*" After he asks and you give it to him, say, "*Put in flour.*" Hold your hand in front of his when he starts to put it in and say, "*Put in?*" Require him to say, "*Put in,*" before he does so.

TECHNIQUES TO USE
IN NEAL'S DIRECTED ACTIVITY TIME

Time: Set aside a regular time each day when you are free from distractions. Limit the whole sequence of activities to about 15 minutes and go through the sequence once each day. The activities should follow the same sequence everyday: 1) Table Time, 2) Movement Time, and 3) Book Time.

Materials: Put all the materials you plan to use in a box. Use them only during this time and keep them put away at other times. Have everything ready before beginning.

Activities: The activities consist of two that are to be at the table (Table Time and Book Time) and one to be carried out in an area where there is room for throwing a ball or dancing (Movement Time). The table should have two chairs (one for each of you). Be consistent in the setting, using the same table and chairs each day. The area for Movement Time does not have to be in the same room but should be in the same place each day.

How to Begin and Carry Out: The first days may be difficult for both of you, as Neal may not be used to such a structured time at home. However, *persist*. He will adjust! Begin by saying, *"Neal, it is table time."* Take his hand and lead him to the table. Point to his chair and say, *"Sit down,"* as you sit in your chair. If he resists, repeat the command using a firm but positive tone of voice; put your hand on his back, sitting him down gently but firmly in his seat. It is important that Neal follow *all* requests that you give him during this time, so give only the essential ones (and ones that you know he can follow).

As soon as he is seated, repeat, *"It is table time."* Have the box of materials in reach. Get these materials and start the activity. When the activity is almost over, tell Neal, *"Table time is almost over."* When finished with the activity, say, *"Table time is over. Now it is movement time."*

Take Neal's hand and walk with him to the area for Movement Time and start that activity. Again when the activity is almost over, tell him so. When finished, say, *"Movement time is over. Now it is book time."* Direct Neal back to his chair at the table and begin the Book Time activity. When this is almost finished, follow the above sequence ending with, *"Book time is over."* Tell Neal, *"We are finished."* Then take his hand and lead him out of the activity area and into whatever household activity is scheduled.

Title: Movement Time

Description:

1. Hold Neal's hand and walk around the room touching each picture saying, *"Here is dog,"* or *"This is dog."* After each time you say it, ask Neal, *"What is this?"* and wait for him to model your response.
2. Stand in the middle of the room and ask Neal, *"Where is dog?"* Then lead him to the correct picture, hold his hand on it, and model, *"Here is dog,"* or *"This is dog."* Wait for him to repeat it.
3. Repeat your previous question for another picture. Wait for Neal to touch the correct picture and give the correct verbal response. Help him as little as possible to complete this.
4. Play the game for several kinds of pictures or until Neal shows signs of becoming restless. For the last round tell him, *"Give me dog,"* and require him to take down the pictures and give them to you.

Suggestions:

1. Praise Neal and/or clap your hands each time he responds correctly.
2. Alternate your phrases as much as possible without changing the structure of the activity. Example: *"Touch dog," "Show me dog," "Point to dog."*
3. Ask for more detail in the pictures as Neal becomes more proficient.
4. After Neal learns the game you could switch roles and have *him* make the requests.

Materials needed:

Simple pictures of animals and objects to some of which Neal has been previously exposed. Use masking tape and put four or five pictures at Neal's height on different walls of the room. Vary the positions each day and substitute new pictures as he learns the old one.

Objectives:

C–8, C–11
A–19

Title: Table Time

Description:

1. Put cards on table individually face up. Point to two matching cards saying, *"This is dog. This is dog."* Pick up these cards, put them together saying, *"This is the same,"* and lay them in front of you.

2. Repeat matching sequence, using the same verbalizations for the remaining sets.

3. Put the cards back on the table and say, *"You do it. It's your turn."* Require Neal to complete the sequence as you did. If necessary, point to the cards, giving the verbalization, and then require him to say it. When he has finished, say, *"Game is over."*

4. If Neal has not tired, repeat the steps.

Materials needed:

Six simple pictures of animals and objects that make three different pairs (for example, two dogs, two cats, and two boats)

Objectives:

A–22

Title: Book Time

Description:

1. Say, *"It is time to cut. Here is paper* (as you hold up paper), *here is line* (as you point to line)." Continue, *"Cut on line* (as you demonstrate)." Repeat, *"On line."*

2. Offer scissors and paper to Neal saying, *"I have paper,"* and requiring him to say, *"I want paper."* Repeat for scissors.

3. Tell Neal, *"Cut on line."* If he does not attempt to follow the line, repeat the instruction as you point to the line. Praise Neal as he cuts.

4. Ask Neal to give back materials, saying, *"Give me____,"* as you hold out your hand.

Materials needed:

1. Paper cut into fourths with a line drawn down the middle of each piece
2. Scissors

Objectives:

C–8
A–24

Title: Book Time

Description:

Complete all steps for preceding card except do not ask Neal to return the paper.

1. Say, *"I have book, . . . I have paste,"* as you hold them up. Require Neal to ask for each.
2. Say, *"Put paste,"* as you turn over one of the papers he has cut.
3. After putting on the paste, say, *"Put here,"* as you point to the first box. Repeat until boxes are filled.
4. Require Neal to return the paste as in Step 4 on the preceding card.
5. Tell Neal, *"I have pencil,"* and require him to ask for it.
6. Tell Neal, *"Write name,"* as you point to one of the pasted cards. Say, *"Make N,"* and continue for all the letters in his name. Give him assistance if he asks for it, but encourage him to do it by himself on the other cards.
7. Repeat Step 6 for other cards or until Neal shows signs of tiring.

Suggestions:
1. Praise Neal for everything, saying, *"Good paper"* or other simple words.
2. Stop after Step 4 if Neal starts to get bored.

Materials needed:

1. Paper cut from preceding activity
2. Paste
3. Homemade "book" with construction paper that has four rectangular boxes drawn on each sheet to correspond with paper Neal has cut

Objectives:

C–8, C–11
A–24

Title: Book Time

Description:

1. Demonstrate drawing of boy, labeling parts as you do so. Example: *"Here is hand,"* etc.

2. Offer Neal paper and pencil, requiring him to ask for them.

3. Say, *"Make circle,"* pointing to his paper. If he takes your hand, require him to ask for help. Then put your hand over his.

4. Repeat for other body parts. Ask him what they are as you draw. Whenever necessary, give him the word for the correct part.

5. Keep it simple. Limit parts to: head, eyes, nose, mouth, hair, body, arms, legs, hands, feet.

Materials needed:

1. Paper
2. Pencil

Objectives:

A-24

Title: Table Time

Description:

1. Put cards on table individually face up. Point to two matching cards saying, *"This is 2. This is 2."* Pick up these cards, put them together saying, *"These are the same,"* and lay them in front of you.

2. Repeat matching sequence, using the same verbalizations for the remaining sets. Afterwards, say, *"Game is over."*

3. Put the cards back on the table and say, *"You do it. It's your turn."* Require Neal to complete the sequence as you did. If necessary, point to the cards, giving the verbalization, and then require him to say it. When he has finished, say, *"Game is over."*

4. If Neal has not tired, repeat the steps.

Materials needed:

Six cards from regular card deck which make three different pairs (for example, two 2s, two 4s, and two 6s)

Objectives:

A–25

Title: Table Time

Description:

1. Put the cards on the table as in Step 1 on the preceding card. Point to two *unmatching* cards, saying, *"This is 2. This is 6."* Hold them together, saying, *These are different."* Then put cards back in their original place, saying, *"Put back. My turn is over."*
2. Say, *"You do it. It's your turn."* Require Neal to imitate Step 1 as you did it. If he has trouble, help him as in the previous card. Say, *"Your turn is over,"* if he does not say it for himself.
3. Say, *"It's my turn."* This time pick a matching set using the verbalizations on the previous card. Keep the matching pair. Then pick two different cards, after which your turn will be over. Then tell Neal that it is his turn.
4. Require Neal to use the correct verbalizations although he can choose to pick either matching or different sets.
5. Take turns until Neal tires. Every time the cards are used up say, *"Game is over."*

Materials needed:

Same as previous card.

Objectives:

C–8, C–11
A–25

Title: Table Time

Description:

1. Put one set of cards on the table. Touch the two identical pictures, saying, *"These are same!"* Then touch the different one, saying, *"This is different."*

2. Say, *"Give me the same cards;"* then, *"Give me the different cards."* You will probably have to help Neal by turning your hand over to refuse the wrong cards. If so, ask again until he gives you the right ones.

3. Repeat for other sets but do not go through the cards more than three times.

Suggestions:

1. Switch the cards around to make new sets.
2. Eliminate Step 2, gradually giving Neal a chance to say, *"This is different,"* or *"These are same,"* after asking him, *"What is this?"*

Material needed:

Sets of three cards with shapes, symbols, and simple designs — two of the cards in each set are the same; the third is different

Objectives:

A–25

Title: Table Time

Description:

1. Hold the turtle, saying, *"This is a turtle."*
2. Put the turtle under the table, saying, *"The turtle is under the table. Where is the turtle?"* Repeat the first statement if necessary; then, require Neal to say, *"Turtle under the table."*
3. Give Neal the turtle and tell him to put it under the table. Example: *"Put the turtle under the table. Show me the turtle under the table."* Ask him where the turtle is as in Step 2.
4. Repeat the same structure for concept but vary the sentences you use as shown in the example in Step 3 to help Neal learn the function of the statements and questions.
5. Use the same procedure for other concepts always pairing the opposites.

Suggestions:

Repeat the structure but have Neal put the turtle under the chair or under a cloth, etc. Also, alternate the turtle with the dog. When using the dog, try putting it on your hand and talking for it. Encourage Neal to do the same when it is his turn.

Materials needed:

1. Dog puppet or toy turtle
2. Box (for *in* and *out*)
3. Concepts to teach: *under, over; in, out; up, down*

Objectives:

A–28

RAY'S HOME PROGRAM

Ray had many skills compared to the other children in the Stage One class. Perhaps his greatest asset was his cuteness, which he used to please adults. This attribute made him especially attractive to his teachers and the adults in his family; yet, it also worked against the natural process of developing independence. He loved being the baby, and others loved to baby him.

His parents were eager and able to be involved with Ray's home program. His mother first worked in the Stage One classroom once a week as a volunteer support teacher. In this way she successfully learned the basic Stage One management techniques. Because of her involvement and available free time, we felt that she and Ray would benefit from a formal, highly structured learning time at home, as well as a program to improve his performance in daily home routines.

Because he was not attempting to help himself in any of the basic self-help activities and because he was not even attempting to communicate verbally, these two areas became the primary objectives for Ray's home program (B-5 and C-3).

DEVELOPMENTAL THERAPY OBJECTIVES (DTORF)

Behavior

B-4: to respond with motor and body responses to complex environmental and verbal stimuli (through imitation "Do this;" through completion of verbal direction; or through minimal participation in activities) given physical intervention and verbal cues

B-5[2]: to actively assist in learning self-help skills (toileting, washing hands, dressing, putting arms in coat when held) (Should be based upon chronological age expectations in combination with developmental expectations. Mastery not essential.)

B-8: to use play materials appropriately, simulating normal play experience (Child plays with toys with awareness of their function, both as representative, real-life objects (play stove for cooking) as well as objects for pretending (play stove turned over makes a castle wall). He does not see toys as objects to be destroyed but as objects that he uses to facilitate his fantasy or to play out real-life situations. If a child has difficulty discriminating reality from fantasy, it would not be appropriate for him to continually pretend.)

Communication

C-3[2]: to respond to verbal stimulus and single object with a recognizable approximation of the appropriate verbal response (Child gives verbal approximation to indicate use or correct answer to question, "What is this?" Object present; function or name acceptable.)

Socialization

S-5: to engage in organized solitary play (with direction from adult if necessary; age-appropriate play not necessary)

The home program given to Ray's mother appears on pages 41–42.

---

[2]Major emphasis.

TO HELP RAY LEARN SELF-HELP SKILLS (B-5)

Ray is learning to actively assist in self-help skills (feeding, drinking, dressing, washing). He should be assisted in practicing these skills daily. We will put off toilet training until there is success with these activities.

1. Ray should assist in dressing and undressing—put on and take off shoes, socks, pants, shirt, coat. A controlled vocabulary should be used when giving commands, reflections, and praise: *"Ray, pull up sock," "Ray is taking off coat,"* and *"Ray is taking off shoes."*
Physical touch and nurturance should be used here as he gets involved.

2. Ray should assist in washing and drying his hands. He loves to feel water, but he is too easily contented with the physical sensation and movement of the water. He should be directed to rub his hands under the water, *"Ray, wash hands in water."* Take his hands and rub them together under the water. *"Ray is washing hands."* Then praise him and provide physical contact. This will make him want to be successful.

3. Ray should have, whenever possible, at least one very spoonable food that can't be pushed or rolled out of the spoon. Examples: applesauce, mashed potatoes, soft foods mashed up so they will be easily spooned. He should be motored in the motion of holding the spoon in his hand and putting it into the food and back up to his mouth. There will be times when he will back his head away, but he should still be put through the motions, making sure the spoon at least touches his lips for him to get the taste. Make sure this motoring is done gently and supportively.

At the present time he should be allowed to continue to eat the more solid foods (bread, meat, etc.) with his fingers. Take the spoon away when he is eating these solids. Do *not* allow him to use or put his fingers in the food that he is expected to spoon. Hold his free hand if necessary, but in a nurturing way. Again use controlled vocabulary directions, reflection, and praise: *"Eat with spoon,"* and *"Good, Ray is eating with spoon."*

RAY'S SPECIAL LEARNING TIME

Set aside 15 to 20 minutes a day during which one parent can be alone with no distractions to put Ray through a regular routine of four activities. This should be done in a part of the house where there is floor space for a play area and a table with two chairs. It is best to have a rug or some other way of defining the play area.

There should be several different manipulative play materials (truck, ball, blocks, form box, etc.) and a particular place for a box or cabinet from which Ray should take out and put back toys.

Each day go through the same routine of four activities: Work Time, Play Time, Exercise Time, and Mouth Time. The cards explain what to do for each activity. We will design new cards for each of these activities whenever you feel that Ray is successful and needs something new.

Title: Work Time

Description:

1. Lead Ray to the table for the activity. Reflect, *"Ray is sitting for work time."* Have three or four different tasks in a box for him to do, and have all the materials ready to be used, one at a time. Examples: form box, puzzle, rings.
2. Take out form box and shake it to attract attention. *"We have box for Ray."* Take out the blocks, keep them yourself, and give them to him one at a time. Commands should be very simple, *"Put in! Put in!"* If he is looking at you instead of his work, tell him to *"Look at it,"* and keep your eye contact while you give him praise.
3. Have him give you the materials when he is finished with them.
4. After he completes all of his task, announce, *"Work time is over."*

Materials needed:

Form box, puzzle, rings or similar materials in a box

Objectives:

B–8
S–5

Title: Play Time

Description:

1. To start activity, announce enthusiastically: *"It's play time! Let's go to the floor for play time."*

2. Move to the area set aside for Play Time. If Ray does not come, say, *"Our play time is on the floor. Come to floor for play time."* If he still does not come, guide him to the play area.

3. Whenever Ray comes to the rug, use verbal praise and physical contact to reward him, *"Good! Ray is on the rug for play time."*

4. Direct him to the toys, using physical touch if necessary. Reward him for going there. He will probably pick up a toy on his own initiative. Reflect, *"Ray has _____ ."* Then have him use the toy appropriately. Interrupt and redirect inappropriate use of the toy, especially spinning and flipping.

5. Using controlled vocabulary, give directions for appropriate use of toy. Example: *"Push truck"* or *Throw ball."* Again reflect what he is doing and reward him with a hug or special smile for doing it.

6. During the activity, have Ray pick out specific toys from where they are kept, saying, *"Pick up _____ ."* Then ask Ray, *"What is this?"* It is important to get some sort of sound from Ray in answer to your question. If need be, have him look at your face by gently turning his face toward yours. Carefully make the word as a model for him. Then ask him again, *"What is this?"*

Materials needed:

A few familiar toys, such as a ball and a truck

Objectives:

B–8
C–3
S–5

Title: Exercise Time

Description:

Lead Ray from the table to the activity area. When giving commands in this activity, the only verbalization used is, *"Do this."* You should have four tasks:
1. Stick hands straight out and bring them together, saying *"Do this."* Repeat about three times, moving him through it if needed. Praise him even if you have to move him through it: *"That's good."*
2. Pat knees.
3. Raise arms.
4. Wave.

Be sure to convey fun and pleasure in doing this together.

Materials needed:

None

Objective:

B–4

Title: Mouth Time

Description:

This activity is designed to help Ray with speech. It will give him different exercises for the mouth to help use mouth muscles. The first two exercises are blowing and licking.

Blowing: Ray should be put through three different blowing exercises:
1. A feather on the end of a string is one he enjoys, and he can see the results of his blowing. You should hold it up and just say, *"Blow,"* and demonstrate it. To help him make the connection, sometimes you say, *"Do this,"* and blow it for him. Reflect, *"Ray is blowing."*
2. Have him blow a floating material with a sail across some water.
3. Use a "party blower" that curls up and makes noises.

Licking: Put peanut butter on a tongue depressor and have Ray lick it off the stick. He will try to put the stick into his mouth. Intervene and say, *"Ray, lick stick."* This will let him know he can get the peanut butter without using his hands.

Materials needed:

Feather, strings, paper or wooden boat, party blower, tongue depressor, and peanut butter

Objectives:

B–4
C–3

A SUBSTITUTE HOME PROGRAM FOR RONALD

Ronald's parents both worked long hours and were not able to conduct any home program for him. As an alternative, a program was designed to be conducted in the day care center where he was kept until 6:00 p.m. each evening. While the day care staff were willing to become involved, they expressed concern over their lack of training and experience in working with a child such as Ronald. For this reason, Ronald's teacher from the Developmental Therapy class visited the day care center in the afternoon twice each week and conducted this program as a demonstration. The head teacher was given the program with objectives and general guidelines. It required setting aside 15 to 20 minutes each afternoon for a highly structured routine, an abbreviated version of the program Ronald had each morning in his Developmental Therapy class at the center.

Eventually the day care staff became more confident and involved. The goal, of course, was to have the day care staff conduct the program every day on their own.

The program consisted of four activities: Play, Work, Exercise ("*do this*"), and Juice and Cookies. One or two other children at the day care center, of similar developmental level, were encouraged to participate. This provided a small group, with the obvious benefits of social interaction, modeling, and imitation.

DEVELOPMENTAL THERAPY OBJECTIVES (DTORF)

Behavior

B-8: to use play materials appropriately, simulating normal play experience (Child plays with toys with awareness of their function, both as representative, real-life objects (play stove for cooking) as well as objects for pretending (play stove turned over makes a castle wall). He does not see toys as objects to be destroyed but as objects which he uses to facilitate his fantasy or to play out real-life situations. If a child has difficulty discriminating reality from fantasy, it would not be appropriate for him to continually pretend.)

B-9: to wait without physical intervention by adult (Verbal support or touch may be used.)

B-10: to participate in sitting activities such as Work Time, Story Time, Talking Time, Snack Time without physical intervention by adult (Child is able to take part in the activities by staying in the activity area, responding to materials, and following teacher's directions, given verbal support or touch by the adult.)

Communication

C-3: to respond to verbal stimulus and single object with a recognizable approximation of the appropriate verbal response (Child gives verbal approximation to indicate use or correct answer to question, "*What is this?*" Object present; function or name acceptable.)

Socialization

S-5: to engage in organized solitary play (with direction from adult if necessary; age-appropriate play not necessary)

(Pre)Academics

A-6: to imitate simple, familiar actions of adult

A-7: to respond by simple discrimination of objects (Child gives correct motor or verbal response to a command such as, "*Give me _____,*" or "*Touch the _____.*" Two different objects presented.)

The substitute home program designed for Ronald appears on page 44.

RONALD'S AFTERNOON PROGRAM

Play Time (about 7 minutes)

This activity should be done in a designated area of the room which should be called the "play area." Ronald should be helped in playing with several different toys in an appropriate way, such as dressing a doll, rocking the doll, turning the handle of the Jack-in-the-box. Help him use toys in the way they were designed. He should be kept in the play area by keeping him interested in the materials. When Play Time is over, he should be required to identify each toy as he puts it away. Example: Have a truck and ball beside each other. Say to Ronald, *"Here is ball. Here is truck. Pick up truck."*

Encourage the children to use the same toys together to simulate normal play.

Work Time (about 5 minutes)

After the toys have been put up, lead Ronald over to the table for Work Time. Start off the activity with a relatively familiar task to ease him into work time successfully (such as the form box, puzzle, or rings). Really build his confidence for the next, more difficult task. The next task should be discriminating among objects, given the names. Example: Have three objects (block, cup, spoon). One at a time show Ronald the object and say, *"Here is block,"* putting emphasis on *"block."* Have Ronald touch the correct object. Repeat for each object.

Next, have all the objects lined up in front of Ronald on the table and say, *"Give me cup."* If he goes for the wrong object say, *"That's spoon. Give me cup."* Point to what you want while you identify it. If he cannot do it, guide his hand to the cup. Praise him and be sure to reflect when he gives you one. Repeat on all objects. After he does this, he should begin discriminating simple pictures of these same objects.

Exercise ("do this") Time (about 2 minutes)

After Work Time is over, have Ronald move to the floor for this activity. In all probability there will not be any problem in getting him to leave the table, but he may deliberately try to run to a different area of the room. If at all possible, limit him to the area of the activity. Ronald loves praise and loves to hear his name called. While moving him to the area you should say very positively and cheerfully, *"Ronald is going to the floor for 'Do This' Time."* If he has already gotten away from you, try to lure him back verbally with a lot of affection and a pleasant, rewarding expression on your face. He is at the point where he likes being involved with you and what's going on, so after saying, *"Ronald, we sit on the floor for 'Do This' Time,"* start the activity with the other child. Most of the time he will come to or near the activity. Go to get him as a last resort.

This activity is to help the children to imitate simple actions of adults. Begin by saying, *"Let's all do this."* Then raise hands up in the air. Give command to each child by name. Move them through it if they cannot do it by themselves. *"Look, Ronald, put hands up."* Repeat this procedure with combing hair, clapping hands, touching tummy, feet, head.

Juice and Cookies Time (about 6 minutes)

This activity is designed especially for language stimulation. Right now Ronald is *very* consistent in giving a long drawn out /k/ sound. He will ask for the cookie this way when it is presented to him. He should still get a cookie when he asks like this, but you should really try to have him make the /ee/ connection. Also, it does not have to be cookies every day. You can vary the foods for stimulation of different sounds. Try apples, yogurt, and raisins. Ronald is not all that excited by juice, but he should still be asked for an /oo/ sound. Ronald is on a nonpreservative diet; therefore, any foods he eats should be entirely natural.

part 4

COMMENTS ABOUT THE DEVELOPMENTAL THERAPY OBJECTIVES FOR STAGES ONE AND TWO

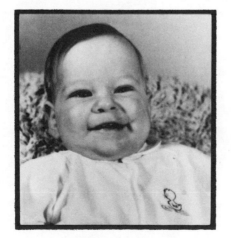

Even after learning the basic procedures for using the Developmental Therapy Objectives Rating Form (DTORF), teachers and parents of CSID children may have difficulty rating a CSID child because of his unusual behavior patterns.[1] The following discussion is offered in the hope that some of the difficulty can be reduced or eliminated by considering the intent of the objectives from a sequential, developmental frame of reference.

Perhaps the most confusing objectives are the first few in each curriculum area (Behavior, Communication, Socialization, and (Pre)Academics). We have seen people rating children too *low* because they see the first objectives as more complex than we had intended. As a general guideline, think of the beginning objectives as reflecting the developmental milestones associated with the first six months of a normal infant's life; yet, remember that severely delayed older children might need to master these same objectives.

The following objectives have been selected for discussion in some depth because they appear to be the ones more frequently misinterpreted. Not all of the objectives seem to need such clarification; therefore, only a few are included in the following discussion. All of the objectives for Stages One and Two are included in Appendix a.

BEHAVIOR

> B-0:   to indicate awareness of a sensory stimulus with any responses away from or toward source of stimulus (in situations with tactile, motor, visual, auditory, taste, or smell stimuli) (Child must have two out of six modalities.)

This objective calls for the most basic indication of awareness of environmental stimuli. The assessment should consider each sensory system and determine 1) which sensory systems are working and.which are not working and 2) which is the preferred sensory modality.

[1] For basic instructions in using the Developmental Therapy Objectives Rating Form (DTORF) see: Combs, C. Developmental therapy curriculum objectives (Chapter 2). *In* Wood, M. M. (ed.) Developmental Therapy, pp. 17–35. University Park Press, Baltimore.

Sensory channels are the child's link to the world, and, if the child is going to learn, he first must be able to receive sensory inputs. If he is not showing awareness of some stimuli (through vision, touch, movement, hearing, taste, or smell), it will be very difficult to organize and teach him. If a child's sensory receiving apparatus is not working normally, he may perceive ordinary stimuli as distorted, frightening, or meaningless. He also may be blind or deaf or have some other profound sensory impairment. Another possibility is that he may choose not to show his awareness. Perhaps he is too confused or alienated to do so.

It may require an extended period of time to assess each sensory channel. By using each type of sensory stimulus, you can begin to see which modality causes a response in the child. This will help you determine the type of stimulus that reaches a particular child. The quality of a child's response is not important when considering this first objective. He may turn away when spoken to, he may shudder when touched, or he may scream when he hears music. In each instance, however, he has shown that he has mastered B-0 if he gives any sort of response to stimuli 90% of the time in each of two modalities.

Your next task is to find a pleasurable way to arouse the child through each of the preferred sensory systems. Later in this text we offer sample techniques and materials, but each child is so different that these ideas are only a starting point. It is more important to find out what arouses your child and what can produce a reaction.

After you determine which sensory channels to focus on, you can begin to explore ways of using each modality to give the child pleasure, hopefully increasing his ability and desire to be aware of his environment. You now have a pathway for relating to the child. Use it to bring him pleasure and to associate you with that pleasure. In short, aim at 1) sensory arousal and 2) building trust and increased ability to respond to the environment. For example, if a child is using taste as his primary modality, then provide many opportunities for tasting foods, and allow the child to explore by taste other materials that would not be harmful to him.

Gradually you can redirect the child's exploration of the world into other sensory modalities. For example, when the child instinctively raises a ball to his mouth, gently redirect the movement to his cheeks. To expand into a sensory modality previously inactive, provide the child with numerous pleasurable opportunities to experience the new sensations. This idea of pairing a modality that is not working well with one that is functioning well is extremely important. For example, teaching a child to become aware that you are speaking to him is often helped by pairing pleasurable touching each time you speak. Keep in mind, however, that a child often receives pleasure from one kind of touch and not another. This is one of your biggest jobs—finding out what gives each child pleasure, increasing his awareness, and then using this knowledge to tune him into both his environment and you.

> B-1: to react to sensory stimulus by attending toward source of stimulus by body response or by looking (in situations using tactile, motor, visual, auditory, taste, or smell stimuli) (Same as Academics A-1.) (Child must have two out of six modalities.)

The difference between B-0 and B-1 is that in B-1 the child's response must be *toward* a stimulus. The response need not be appropriate, but it must be a movement in that direction. For example, a child who is "freaking out" on a toy, spinning the wheels with his fingers and holding it in front of his eyes, is not behaving appropriately. However, in order to master this objective, a child only needs to react *toward* the source of stimulus (e.g., toy), using visual, tactile, or motor modalities.

Through careful observation and the presentation of a rich, varied environment (with materials and personal contact), you can discover which modalities a child prefers to use. With this knowledge you can plan ways to obtain the child's attention and then begin to build skills.

For the child who is not reacting to his environment or who is reacting negatively or bizarrely, you must use great skill in presenting stimuli that will generate a reaction toward the stimuli and not away from it. This may mean finding creative ways to provide pleasurable sensory experiences and devising new ways to use your body, voice, and touch. Much experimenting and creativity on the part of a teacher and parent is usually necessary because what

arouses one child toward a stimulus may frighten another child away.

> B-2: to respond to stimulus by sustained attending toward source of stimulus (continued looking at object or person after initial stimulus-response has occurred) (Same as Academics A-2.)

This objective often is defined by different people using different criteria and can be difficult to rate. It is intended, however, to rate *only* a child's capacity for remaining aware of a stimulus after the initial stimulus has been given. It implies psychological awareness but should not be confused with "attention span" as we usually think of it in school-age children. In general, CSID children have difficulty with this objective because they cannot maintain sustained attending long enough to get meaning and sensory feedback from their own responses.

> B-3: to respond spontaneously to simple environmental stimulus with a motor behavior; object, person, sound (Same as Academics A-3.)

This objective concerns the child's use of muscles in response to a specific stimulus. It implies a spontaneous, unassisted motor behavior. As with B-0, this objective does not specify that the response be a positive one. Nor does the objective require a complicated or a skilled act. Keep in mind that this objective includes motor activity comparable to that of the nonhandicapped infant under one year of age.

> B-4: to respond with motor and body responses to complex environmental and verbal stimuli (through imitation "Do this;" through completion of verbal direction; or through minimal participation in activities) given physical intervention and verbal cues (Same as Academics A-4.)

The word "complex" tends to throw people off the track with this objective. The intent is that there is more than one step involved from the stimulus to the response and that the response is *slightly* more complicated than at the B-3 level. This objective includes "minimal participation . . . given physical intervention and verbal cues." Included in this objective are 1) the large muscle activities usually associated with nonhandicapped children up to about 18 months of age and 2) simple, imitative activities performed with physical or verbal assistance from another person.

This objective should not be confused with B-10, B-11, or B-12 which are concerned with various types of *participation in activities*. For a child who *can* move his muscles for purposes of accomplishing something but is obviously resisting the routine or the testing limits, or is unable to organize himself sufficiently, B-10, B-11, or B-12 would be the more accurate objective.

> B-5: to actively assist in learning self-help skills (toileting, washing hands, dressing, putting arms in coat when held) (Should be based upon chronological age expectations in combination with developmental expectations. Mastery not essential.)

When considering the broad category of self-help skills (as this objective does), the key is *active assistance*. The objective reflects involvement in the activity on the child's part. It is not intended to require mastery of the activities.

Problems surrounding toileting and feeding skills are often critical to the adjustment of a young CSID child within his family. We are often asked why we do not have specific objectives for these activities. Perhaps we should; however, it has been our experience that these activities are actually made up of many processes that are included in other objectives. For example, to master control of bladder and bowel, a child must be aware of the bathroom equipment and physical sensations in his body (B-1). He must be able to attend for enough time to complete the task (B-2), and must be able to connect the stimulus with the expected motor behavior (B-3). In addition to the Behavior objectives there are a series of Communication and Socialization objectives that are involved, such as responding to verbal reminders (C-2) and eventually communicating the need to an adult (C-5). Because these processes are so uniquely combined within each child, we prefer to consider toileting and feeding skills as two among a number of activities the young CSID child is learning. With this approach, we have found that both skills will emerge by the time the child has completed most of the Stage One objectives.

> B-8: to use play materials appropriately, simulating normal play experience (Child plays with toys with awareness of their function, both as representative, real-life objects (play stove for cooking) as well as objects for pretending (play stove turned over

makes a castle wall). He does not see toys as objects to be destroyed but as objects that he uses to facilitate his fantasy or to play out real-life situations. If a child has difficulty discriminating reality from fantasy, it would not be appropriate for him to continually pretend.)

As a general guideline, this objective is comparable to the two- to three-year-old level of play.

The nature of a child's play is important in this objective. The child should be able to play with a variety of materials. There should be evidence also that the child is using at least some of the play material in a symbolic representation of real life. Climbing on a jungle gym is a good illustration. A child who is *working* on this objective (but has not mastered it) might be able to climb on the apparatus (which indicates success with objective A-5). When this child extends his use of the equipment into make believe (for example, that it is his house), he has demonstrated this objective in one area of play.

> B-12: to spontaneously participate in activities without physical intervention (Verbal support or touch may be used, but child indicates some personal initiative to participate in every activity except transitions.)

Spontaneous, personal initiative is the key to this objective. It is specifically placed as the last behavior objective for Stage Two because it indicates that a child is, of his own volition, engaging in activities and routines. It indicates that a child has developed some self-monitoring skills and can continue through an entire activity without a great amount of touch and with no physical intervention. B-12 cannot be mastered without first mastering B-10 and B-11.

Because spontaneous participation often is so difficult to accomplish, B-10 and B-11 may require considerable time and work before B-12 is introduced as a major program objective. These objectives can be distinguished from B-12 in two major ways: 1) B-12 applies to all of the activities, whereas B-10 and B-11 apply to two specific categories of activity, and 2) in B-12 the initiative for participation has shifted to the child, whereas in B-10 and B-11 the initiative for participation still comes from the teacher. One good indicator of this difference is the amount of touch and verbal structuring required for successful participation in B-10 and B-11. The amount necessary is significantly reduced in B-12.

COMMUNICATION

C-0:   to produce sounds (Child must vocalize several sounds for social or adaptive expression.)[2]

The most basic form of communication for many CSID children is simply producing undifferentiated sounds which often appear to be meaningless. Consider carefully the context in which the child's sound occurs. We have noticed that sometimes sounds are *social* and sometimes *adaptive*. Social sounds occur when a child makes sounds to other people. Two of the most typical social sound patterns are those of pleasure (such as "*ya, ya, ya*") and those of anger (often produced with a scream). The child usually is trying to express feelings and may or may not convey that he wants to share this with others. The adaptive sounds are distinctly different, not yet directed toward people but signifying differentiation among situations. Often these adaptive sounds have several clear patterns that change from activity to activity. To master this objective, a child's sound patterns need not be consistent. However, if a child is using jargon, word approximations or words (even out of context), he has mastered this objective.

C-2:   to respond to verbal stimulus with a motor behavior (Object present; teacher does not use gestures.)

The quality of the expected motor response for this objective is similar to that of B-3. However, the stimulus that elicits the response is distinctly a verbal one. The intent with this objective is to ensure that the child is mentally connecting simple words with basic motor responses. With mastery of this objective, the child is beginning to understand that words signify things, actions, and people. He may not know how to produce the words clearly or what to do when he hears them, but he is aware that language can represent his environment. This may be thought of as the first indications of receptive language and is usually noted in a nonhandicapped child around six months of age.

A few CSID children may already have developed rather sophisticated jargon or private language systems of their own. If the system is not used

to communicate and if the child does not respond when spoken to, then this objective has not been mastered.

C-3:   to respond to verbal stimulus and single object with a recognizable approximation of the appropriate verbal response[3] (Child gives verbal approximation to indicate use or correct answer to question, "*What is this?*" Object present; function or name acceptable.)

A child should have several sound approximations that are used consistently in several activities in order to demonstrate mastery of this objective.

The question also comes up about the meaning of "recognizable." To whom is the child's sound recognizable? This is a difficult question because people close to the child often rely on situational clues, gestures, body posture, and routines to assist in the interpretation of a sound as a meaningful approximation. The standard we suggest is that the child's approximations should be consistent, meaningful symbols to the child and to those who know him. In this case, a stranger might not necessarily understand the approximation, but the teachers and parents could consider this objective mastered.

This same standard for "recognizable" applies to C-4. The major difference between C-3 and C-4 is that in the latter objective the child *spontaneously* produces the approximation.

C-5:   to produce recognizable single words in several activities, to obtain a desired response from adult, or to label object for adult (e.g., "*water*" instead of "*wa-wa*" for water) (Verbal cues may be used.)

This objective represents the first milestone in which single words can be recognized by others (such as strangers). Either labeling an object or situation or

---

[2]When a child is using words, C-0 is automatically marked as mastered regardless of content or degree of meaningfulness.

[3]Some CSID children are unable to develop oral communication skills even though they seem to have an inner language system. This is particularly evident among older CSID children. Many authorities recommend a total communication effort involving signing and/or a communication board along with experiences to produce oral language. When a child can use an alternative communication form to demonstrate mastery of communication objectives, we suggest that he be rated as having mastered the objective. However, this sign (X̸), to indicate an alternative communication modality, is used. Also, you will want to continue working for oral language.

demanding something of an adult is typical. If the child has some clear words but uses them privately rather than communicating his needs or labeling for another person, he would need to work on this objective.

C-6 is similar to C-5, except that it specifically requires that the word expressions be directed toward another child. This is often difficult for a CSID child and may require considerable planning and effort after C-5 has been mastered.

> C-7: to produce a meaningful, recognizable sequence of words in several activities (without a model) to obtain a desired response from adults or children, or to label (Gestures or verbal clues may be used.)

The word "meaningful" was included in this objective (and also in C-8) to distinguish relevant, organized language from bizarre, out-of-touch, or fantasy talk. If repetitions of TV commercials or other fantasy talk dominate the child's speech, he still needs to work on the objective. However, a child can master this objective while occasionally using jargon, fantasy talk, or TV commercials.

The question comes up as to whether or not sequences of words need to be used with adults or children for mastery of this objective. We feel that it can be used with either. While difficult for many CSID children to master, this objective is essential if advanced socialization and communication skills with adults and peers are to be obtained in the future.

> C-8: to answer a child's and adult's questions or requests with recognizable, meaningful, relevant word(s) (Response does not have to be accurate or constructive.)

This objective gets at the process of understanding language enough to answer questions with understandable words. Mastery of this objective indicates receptive understanding translated into expressive output. The objective is not referring to the quality of the response nor does it intend to imply a wide range of answers to questions.

This objective also states that "the responses do not have to be accurate or constructive." The intent is that responses of yelling, negative words, or incorrect information should not penalize the child's mas-

tery of the objective. *Processes* with both adults and children are the aspects to be obtained.

> C-9: to exhibit a receptive vocabulary no more than two years behind chronological age expectations (as indicated by the Peabody Picture Vocabulary Test (PPVT) or other means)

If there is any doubt as to whether or not this objective is mastered, a good way to assess it is to use the Peabody Picture Vocabulary Test.

> C-10: to label simple feelings in pictures, dramatic play, art, or music: sad, happy, angry, afraid (by gesture or word)

This objective refers only to recognizing the simplest expressions of feelings portrayed explicitly in pictures, characterizations, or art work. A child does not have to use words at all to master this objective. Some children point, others gesture, and some simply label with a word. The important thing to emphasize is that this objective does not intend that a child express his own feelings or those of others.

> C-11: to use simple word sequences to command or request of another child or adult in ways acceptable to classroom procedures (Bizarre language content or socially inappropriate word sequences are not acceptable; behavior is not a consideration.)

The question often comes up as to which objective represents the point at which to focus on the correct use of the first person pronoun. If a child is still using the pronoun incorrectly when this objective becomes a focus, now is the appropriate time to work on it.

This objective represents the first major communication milestone at which time appropriate syntax is expected. It is important to note also that while bizarre language, inappropriate pronouns, or meaningless ideas are not accepted, inappropriate behavior should not influence your rating of a child on this communication objective.

SOCIALIZATION

The first three socialization objectives (S-1 through S-3) represent a sequence involving the emerging awareness of others. The type of responses indicating an acceptable level of mastery may be passive and usually is covert with CSID children. These responses can involve either a child or an adult.

> S-4: Child interacts with adult nonverbally to meet needs

This objective is a milestone for some CSID children. It reflects an active, deliberate movement on the child's part to become involved with an adult. The movement does not need to be positive or well organized. Sometimes a CSID child will demonstrate mastery of this objective by deliberate attacks on the teacher. The important point is that awareness and arousal have occurred.

> S-5: to engage in organized solitary play (with direction from adult if necessary; age-appropriate play not necessary)

It may be easy to confuse this objective with B-6, which focuses on a child's independent movement in seeking a play material, or B-8, which is concerned with the use of play materials in a manner approaching imaginative or symbolic play. S-5 is the step in the play sequence between B-6 and B-8. It focuses on the purposeful (in contrast to random) manipulation of play materials. The intent is that the child demonstrates simple cognitive organization (sensory-motor) through the material. Even though it is included in the Socialization objectives, this objective does not require the involvement of others. It is the readiness step, the preliminary, to future social play.

> S-6: to respond to adult's verbal and nonverbal requests to come to him (Child moves next to adult and looks at him, and child accepts adult's touch.)

This objective should not be confused with your attempts to control a child. The intent is to reflect a child's *willingness* to accept your attempts at social interaction. The best example of mastery of this objective is when the adult opens her arms to hug a child and the child responds to accept the hug. To see where mastery of this objective will lead, refer to S-12.

> S-7: to demonstrate understanding of single verbal requests or directions given directly to child (Adult does not use gestures.)

On first glance there may seem to be much similarity between this objective and B-4. Perhaps the easiest way to differentiate these objectives is by considering 1) the amount of intervention and support needed by the child to be able to perform the request and 2) the form the request takes. In B-4 the desired response is elicited from the child with a direct or indirect verbal statement, and the teacher provides the child with physical intervention and assistance when needed to complete the response. In contrast, S-7 is concerned with the child's ability to respond with understanding to a verbal direction without any assistance.

> S-8: to produce recognizable single words or signs in several activities to obtain a desired response from adult or to label for adult (e.g., "*water*" instead of "*wa-wa*" for water) (Verbal cues may be used.)

In earliest forms of these objectives, C-5, C-6, and C-7 were the same as S-8, S-9, and S-10. This was because of the vital part that communication plays in social relationships. However, a few CSID children do not develop oral communication skills, and this cross-listing of objectives penalized them in both Communication and Socialization.

In current revisions, the objectives in Socialization (S-8, S-9, and S-10) were modified to include "signs" as an acceptable means to communicate with others. We feel that this gives a more accurate picture of a CSID child's development in the area of socialization when he has learned to express his needs to others through signs.

> S-11: to exhibit a beginning emergence of self (indicated by any of these: age-approximate human figure drawing; gesturing pleasure at one's work; use of personal pronoun (I, me, or my); or looking at self in mirror)

A CSID child may take a long time to develop a full awareness of self. However, the developmental milestone that is reflected in this objective is the beginning point of self-awareness.

Notice that use of the personal pronoun is an acceptable criterion. It is important to refer also to C-8 when the correct use of pronouns becomes a focus for communication. If you are teaching a child who does not use the personal pronoun, you should hold off on making it a major focus of his program until he is ready for C-8. We have found that S-11 can be accomplished in a more satisfactory and efficient way by mirror play, satisfying interpersonal exchanges with adults, and other socializing experiences.

> S-12: to seek contact with adult spontaneously (Child moves next to adult or touches him.)

The foundation for accomplishing this objective can be traced back to mastery of S-6. Mastery of this objective also may be a result of mastery of C-12 at which point the child exchanges minimal information with an adult on his own initiative.

This objective in combination with S-11 is a milestone in socialization, because together they represent the accomplishment of the Stage One goal of trusting adults and trusting oneself.

> S-13: to participate spontaneously in specific parallel activities with another child using similar materials but not interacting

This objective is the first in a series of steps toward active peer relationships. By focusing on parallel play with another child that does not demand social skills for interacting, this objective readies the child for interactive play. The next step in the sequence is S-15, which reflects minimal movement toward another child. The culmination of the sequence occurs in S-17 and S-18 when the child learns to interact with others both in organized classroom activities and in less organized play activities. Parallel play is defined as occurring when a child engages in an activity near another child, using similar materials and indicating awareness of the child but not interacting.

It may be helpful to you to contrast B-10, B-11, and B-12 with S-17 and S-18. The Behavior objectives emphasize social interaction to enable participation in activities. In contrast, the Socialization objectives focus especially on interaction with other children. With these differences in emphasis, it is easy to see how a CSID child might more easily master the Behavior objectives than those in Socialization.

ACADEMICS

The first four objectives in (Pre)Academics are the same in Behavior, B-1 through B-4. The cross-listing is used to convey the notion of a sensorimotor foundation to learning. Without these four basic milestones, a child will have enormous difficulty progressing in academic tasks. These basic sensorimotor processes involve 1) functioning sensory receptors, 2) attending, and 3) motor responses.

A-5 refines this first phase of (Pre)Academics by introducing fine and gross motor skills associated generally with the nonhandicapped two-year-old. The importance of motor skills as a child's tools for learning should not be overlooked. For this reason, these skills are woven into the (Pre)Academic objectives. A-13 reflects gross motor skills associated with the typical three- or four-year-old, and A-16 includes fine motor skills for this same stage of development. Fine motor skills become increasingly proficient about the five-year level (A-24) as do the gross motor skills (A-29). With these skills a child has the tools to continue learning.

> A-6: to imitate simple, familiar actions of adult

Imitation is one of a child's most important tools for expanding his skills and concepts. This objective requires a child to watch and respond. Watching and responding are necessary steps to use each time a new task is presented. These imitating steps also provide a means to try out new learning and to receive feedback. For these reasons we include imitating among (Pre)Academic milestones.

> A-7: to respond by simple discrimination of objects (Child gives correct motor or verbal response to a command such as, "*Give me* _____," or "*Touch the* _____.") (Two different objects presented.)

This objective requires the simple association of words with objects. A child demonstrates understanding of concepts by correctly choosing an appropriate object. This achievement begins a series of increasingly abstract steps in learning: A-11, matching identical objects; A-12, labeling pictures or objects; A-14, matching identical pictures; A-15, naming body parts; A-17, naming colors; A-18, using objects; A-19, recognizing details in pictures; A-20, recognizing an object that is different in a set of three objects; A-22, recognizing pictures that are the same and different; A-26, categorizing; and A-28, demonstrating understanding of opposites.

> A-21: to count with one-to-one correspondence to five

This objective is the first in the series related to enumeration and, eventually, math. This objective reflects a child's understanding that each object counted represents one count.

Rote counting is not included as an objective because it does not seem to be a necessary step in the sequence of learning about numbers. The counting objectives are separated rather arbitrarily into 1–5 (A-21) and 5–10 (A-23). This is done to limit the amount of input the child receives as he first learns one-to-one counting.

These first two steps are followed later by A-30, which begins concrete operations with groups of objects to five.

A-27: to write a recognizable approximation of first name without assistance (Adult may initiate request; no model used.)

The readiness skills a child must have mastered before working on this objective are included specifically in A-22, A-24, and A-25. Until a child has mastered these, it is usually futile to attempt a major effort to teach him to write his first name from memory.

A-31: to listen to storytelling

In the preceding discussion of the (Pre)Academic objectives, you may have noticed how several learning modalities have been expanded and then interwoven in the sequence of objectives. The (Pre)Academic objectives at Stages One and Two are aimed at visual perception, fine and gross motor skills, concept building through objects and pictures, language, and symbols. This last objective reflects the process of *listening,* which was not developed directly in previous objectives. It grows indirectly from attending and imitating activities. However, it is an essential tool for learning. For some CSID children, listening (the auditory channel) develops without special emphasis; for others, it will require a concentrated emphasis if the development of the listening objective is to function as a useful process at all.

The intent of this objective is not appropriate behavior or knowledge of the story content; rather, it focuses on a child's ability to maintain mental attention in a situation that is essentially verbal and moderately abstract.

SUMMARY

Figures 1–4 trace the objectives for Stages One and Two through each of the four curriculum areas. These simplified, graphic summaries are intended to provide an index to the general scope and sequence of the developmental milestones included in the Developmental Therapy curriculum for young CSID children. The circled numerals correspond to the objectives contained in the Appendix. The skill areas in the left-hand margins are broad, general categories for the wide range of specific objectives.

You can see a gradual but distinct difference in the clustering of skills between Stages One and Two in Behavior, Communication, and Socialization. However, in the (Pre)Academic domain a less distinct clustering is evident. Here the interweaving of objectives among the skill areas is more pronounced, and several of the skill areas in (Pre)Academics contain objectives at both stages. This reflects the increasing complexity of materials and tasks from tangible, concrete (sensorimotor) learning to semi-abstract (preoperational) learning.

Finally, it is important to emphasize that the Developmental Therapy objectives, while they provide significant check points for documenting child progress, are only the major milestones for social and emotional development. There are many other small, sequential steps occurring between these key objectives. The identification and sequencing of these interim steps can be accomplished most effectively by each child's own teachers and parents, thereby individualizing the developmental process for every child.

Awareness

Attending

Simple motor responses

Complex motor responses (self-help)

Using play materials

Participating in activities

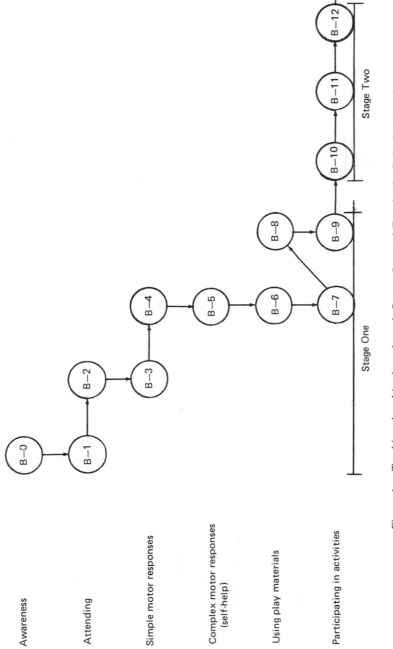

Stage One

Stage Two

On to Stage Three

Figure 1. Tracking the objectives through Stages One and Two in the Behavior domain.

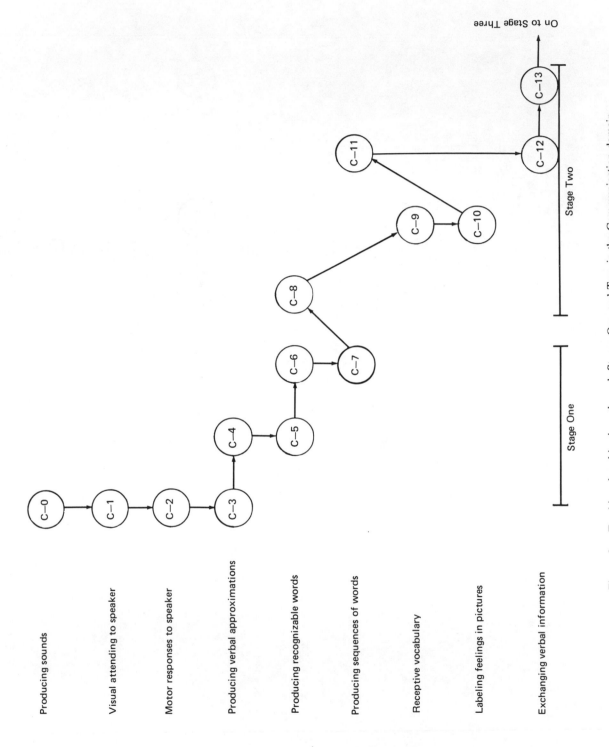

Producing sounds

Visual attending to speaker

Motor responses to speaker

Producing verbal approximations

Producing recognizable words

Producing sequences of words

Receptive vocabulary

Labeling feelings in pictures

Exchanging verbal information

Figure 2. Tracking the objectives through Stages One and Two in the Communication domain.

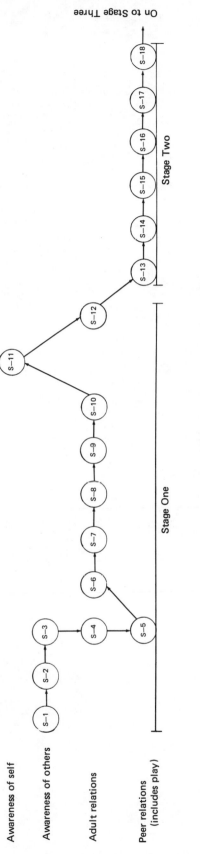

Figure 3.   Tracking the objectives through Stages One and Two in the Socialization domain.

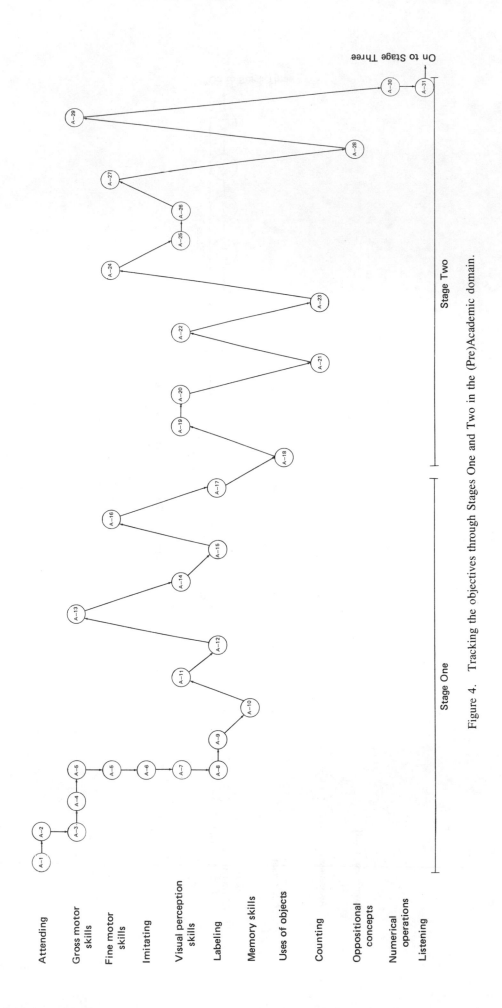

Figure 4. Tracking the objectives through Stages One and Two in the (Pre)Academic domain.

part 5
SAMPLE LEARNING EXPERIENCES

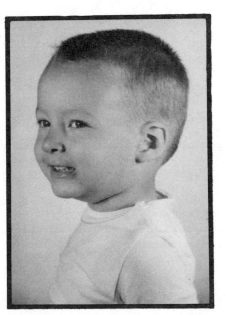

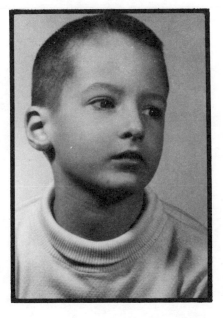

PLAY TIME

CSID Learning Experience/Play Time

Developmental Therapy Objective B-3/to respond spontaneously to a simple environmental stimulus with a motor behavior

Area	Behavior	***Cross-Reference Objectives***	
Stage	I	Behavior	4, 6–8
Name	Ball Bounce	Communication	3–5
		Socialization	3–5, 8
		Academics	3–8

Materials/Special Instructions
Large rubber ball

Support Teacher
Follow the lead teacher's instructions with another child.

LEAD TEACHER

I. **Introduction:** Energetically bounce the ball several times. *"Bounce ball! Bounce ball!"*

II. **Step-by-step:**
1. Show the children the ball, say while bouncing the ball in front of each child, *"Ball! Bounce ball."*
2. Offer the ball to a child. *"Sue, bounce ball."*
3. If a child is reluctant to touch the ball, hold the ball and have the child pat it as you repeat, *"ball."*
4. Stand behind the child and hold the ball with her.
5. Bounce the ball gently with the child, repeating, *"Bounce ball."*

III. **Ending:** Bounce the ball to the toy cabinet, saying, *"Bye-bye ball!"* Bounce the ball into the cabinet and shut the door. You may also direct the children to help by saying, *"Reginald, bounce ball into cabinet."*

IV. **Suggestions:** With children who can bounce the ball themselves, only a verbal request is needed. Encourage the children to *"Throw ball,"* *"Roll ball,"* and *"Kick ball."* Take care to emphasize each process verbally and to respond enthusiastically when a child makes any attempts.

CSID Learning Experience/Play Time

Developmental Therapy Objective B-4/to respond with motor and body responses to complex environmental and verbal stimuli

Area Behavior *Stage:* I *Name:* See-Saw	*Cross-Reference Objectives* Behavior 0–3, 6 Communication 0–5 Socialization 1–3, 5–7 Academics 1–2, 4, 6, 8–9
Materials See-saw	*Support Teacher* If needed, the support teacher will stay near other end of see-saw to assist the child and keep him on it if he is reluctant to do so. Once the child is situated, the support teacher moves to the other children in the room, helping them stay organized at play.

LEAD TEACHER

I. **Introduction:** *"Hi! Let's play see-saw."* Teacher then begins playing with the see-saw very deliberately, making it look irresistable. *"What is this? See-saw!"*

II. **Step-by-step:**
1. *"Reginald, sit on see-saw!"* Encourage verbalization using controlled vocabulary.
2. Direct another child to sit on the other end of the see-saw. You may have to pick the child up at first against his wishes to show him what you mean. Hold him on the see-saw for a moment. Then let him down if he doesn't enjoy it.
3. *"Let's see-saw."* Move the see-saw up and down.

III. **Ending:** Say, *"Stop see-saw!"* Assist children in getting off. *"Good see-sawing."*

IV. **Suggestions:** Try to get both children to look at each other. Show the children how to push the see-saw up and down. For the child with limited verbal skills, you may concentrate only on *"see-saw"* and /s/ for weeks. After the child learns *"see-saw"* concentrate on *"up"* and *"down."*

CSID Learning Experience/Play Time

Developmental Therapy Objective B-8/to use play materials appropriately, simulating normal play experience

Area Behavior *Stage:* II *Name:* Fun with Trucks	*Cross-Reference Objectives:* Behavior 11 Communication 8, 12–13 Socialization 13, 17–18 Academics 18
Materials Small toy cars and trucks	*Support Teacher* Interact with the children to get them involved with the cars and trucks. *"Mike, what do you have?"* Give the child the correct word if he is not able to respond: *"Truck, Mike has the truck!"*

LEAD TEACHER

I. **Introduction:** "Drive" the truck on floor, enthusiastically making truck sounds. Say, *"Look out! Here comes the truck!"*

II. **Step-by-step:**
1. Ask children individually if they want to drive a truck and require them to say, *"Truck,"* before giving it.
2. Encourage children to push trucks to various spots in the room (example: to visit the support teacher).

III. **Ending:** After announcing that play is over, say, *"Time for all trucks to drive into the cabinet,"* and model by putting yours in the cabinet.

IV. **Suggestions:** For a higher level class introduce a gas station, houses, etc. Get items to carry in the trucks such as sticks for logs, cotton balls, and small pretend milk cartons. Encourage communication with peers and adults by having the children take these items to others and "sell" them, etc. Another way to encourage language is to have the children call each other from their trucks on imaginary CB radios.

CSID Learning Experience/Play Time

Developmental Therapy Objective S-7/to demonstrate understanding of single verbal requests or directions given directly to child

Area Socialization
Stage: I
Name: End of Play Time

Cross-Reference Objectives:
Behavior   3–4, 7, 10–12
Communication   1–2, 8
Socialization   1–4, 6
Academics   3–4, 6–7

Materials/Special Instructions

Announce that play time is *almost* over. Make sure each child hears this because it will be hard for some children to end play time. Once the child realizes that he must stop his exciting activity but can expect the same fun the next day, he will be willing to end play time.

Support Teacher

Give verbal support and praise to the children for following requests. Assist them when needed in putting toys away. If a child goes away from the area or stands idly by, not involving himself with clean up, encourage him to help by picking up a toy, giving it to him, and directing him to the cabinet.

LEAD TEACHER

I. Introduction: *"Play time is over. Now it's time to put toys away."*

II. Step-by-step:

1. A doll may be lying on the floor. In a matter-of-fact manner but with the expectation that the children are willing to respond, verbalize, *"Sue, put doll in bed. Mike, put truck in cabinet."*

2. Give each child a specific toy to put away. If another child intervenes, say, *"Joey wants to help Mike put truck in cabinet."*

3. Observe each child to see if he follows the request without intervention. If child does not follow the request, assist him. Then verbalize what the child has done. *"Mike put truck in cabinet! Good boy!"*

4. If he continues to need help each day, gradually cut back on the amount of help given to see when he can follow through on his own. Pull back more and more until he does it alone, always verbalizing, always praising.

III. Ending: When all the toys have been put away, say, *"Look! Toys are put away and play time is over."*

IV. Suggestions: Make sure each child has an opportunity to participate in the clean up. Someone will probably go directly to the table. Bring the child back (still positively) and verbalize *"Time to put toys in cabinet. Then we go to table."* If another child doesn't want play time to end and starts a temper tantrum, say, *"It's hard to put truck away, Mike, but play time is over."* Then help Mike put the truck away.

CSID Learning Experience/Play Time

Developmental Therapy Objective S-13/to participate spontaneously in specific parallel activities near another child, using similar materials but not interacting

Area: Socialization
Stage: II
Name: Going Fishing

Cross-Reference Objectives:
Behavior   6, 8, 11–12
Communication   3, 4, 6–8
Socialization   4, 6, 8–10, 15–16
Academics   3, 6, 8–9, 16, 18

Materials/Special Instructions
Playskool wood rocking boat or large blocks that can be arranged in the shape of a boat. If blocks are used, encourage the children to help build the boat. Give each child a fishing pole with line and hook (gem clip or blunt wire for hook). Make fish from construction paper. Be sure to attach a hook or loop to the fish so the hook on the pole can catch them.

Support Teacher
Direct the children to the boat and encourage individual verbalizations. Watch out for poles to avoid accidents or confusion. Assist the lead teacher with putting fish on the hooks. Touch a child's pole and ask, *"What is this?"* or *"Pole! You say it. Pole!"* Then, *"What did you catch?"* Wait for a response. If the child doesn't respond, say, *"Fish! You say it. Fish!"*

LEAD TEACHER

I. **Introduction:** Show the children a fishing pole and say, *"What is this?"* After they have identified it, say, *"Let's go fishing in a boat!"*

II. **Step-by-step:**
1. If the rocking boat is not available, give the children the large blocks. *"Let's build a boat!"*
2. Encourage all children to get into the boat. Say excitedly, *"We are going fishing! I have a pole for Joey,"* etc.
3. When all the children are in the boat, place the fish on the floor and urge the children to catch them. *"Joey, let's catch a fish!"*
4. Put the fish on the hooks for children who are unable to manipulate their poles and catch fish themselves. Be sure each child catches at least one fish.

5. Elicit language from each child. *"Wow! Look at Joey's fish. Maria, catch a big fish."* Encourage the children to speak to each other.

III. **Ending:** When using the rocking boat, a good ending for this activity is to announce, *"Our fishing trip is over for today. Time to go back to shore."* With the support teacher's help, rock the boat back and forth, sliding it across the floor. Sing "Row, Row, Row Your Boat," encouraging the children to sing along. If the rocking boat was not used, pretend to row the block boat.

IV. **Suggestions:** In addition to fishing trips, the rocking boat is a good toy for pretend boat rides and boat races.

CSID Learning Experience/Play Time

Developmental Therapy Objective A-6/to imitate simple, familiar acts of adults

Area: Academics
Stage: I
Name: Bean Bag Throw

Cross-Reference Objectives:
Behavior   0–4
Communication   0–3, 5
Socialization   1–2, 8
Academics   1–6

Materials/Special Instructions
Bean bags and a box

Support Teacher
Direct the children to the lead teacher and to the other children. Keep the children focusing on what the lead teacher is doing. For those children who are just beginning to learn to sit, do this activity with each child for only a moment so the others do not have to wait long.

LEAD TEACHER

I. **Introduction:** Announce the activity and sit on the floor. Show the children the bean bag saying *"Bean bag!"* Then throw the bean bag into the big box, verbalizing, *"Throw in box!"*

II. **Step-by-step:**
1. Ask each child to throw the bean bag.
2. For children with verbal skills, ask, *"What do you want, Joey?"* Child responds *"Bean bag"* or simply makes a /b/ sound.
3. Have the child stand up and throw the bean bag into the box verbalizing *"Throw in box."*
4. Praise the child and direct him to the floor and give another child a turn.

5. Move the child who cannot respond to directions through the activity by putting a bag in his hand and throwing it in. Say, *"Good. You* (or *Joey*) *threw in!"*

III. **Ending:** When the bean bags are all in the box, say, *"Stop! Bean bags in box."*

IV. **Suggestions:** Place a two-foot strip of masking tape on the floor. Have the children try to throw the bean bag on the strip or over it. Make a circle, triangle, or square with tape. Have the children throw bean bags inside the figures.

HELLO TIME

CSID Learning Experience/Hello Time

Developmental Therapy Objective B-1/to react to sensory stimulus by attending toward source of stimulus by body response or by looking

Area: Behavior *Stage:* I *Name:* Balloon Play	*Cross-Reference Objectives:* Behavior 2–3 Communication 1–2 Socialization 1, 3 Academics 1–3, 5, 15
Materials/Special Instructions Several large, round, brightly colored balloons	*Support Teacher* As always, lead and support teachers need to have a clear understanding ahead of time of what their strategies will be with each child within the framework of their respective roles. Generally, in this activity you, as support, help direct attention to the lead teacher's actions. Show excitement with your animation, and help individual children to sustain attending behavior and to touch and explore the balloon. You might repeat the words that are used and help guide a child's hand in pushing the balloon.

LEAD TEACHER

I. **Introduction:** Blow up a balloon and let go of it, saying, "*Balloon!*" As the balloon releases the air, it will spin around and land. This should attract the children's attention and cause them to follow the motion of the balloon with their eyes or their bodies. Repeat.

II. **Step-by-step:**
1. Blow up a balloon and knot it.
2. Bounce the balloon up in the air in view of all. "*Bounce balloon!*"
3. Allow the children to try keeping the balloon up in the air. "*Push balloon, bounce balloon!*"

III. **Ending:** Unknot balloon and let it go, saying, "*Balloon gone!*" Or, let one of the children release it.

IV. **Suggestions:** Use the controlled vocabulary frequently and include the color of the balloon in the vocabulary for more advanced children. Have another balloon available in case one pops. If you feel the children will not be frightened, deliberately break the balloon (preparing the children in advance) and include the vocabulary word "*break.*" Encourage the children to touch the balloon.

CSID Learning Experience/Hello Time

Developmental Therapy Objective B-1/to react to sensory stimulus by attending toward source of stimulus by body response or by looking

Area: Behavior	**Cross-Reference Objectives:**
Stage: I	Behavior 0–4, 7
Name: Bubbles	Communication 1–2
	Socialization 1–4
	Academics 1–4

Materials/Special Instructions	**Support Teacher**
Jar of soap bubbles	Be a model for enthusiasm. Use the lead teacher's phrases with individual children. Help the children sit in their own chairs and attend to the bubbles. Say, *"Bubbles!"* to each child excitedly. Direct them toward the lead teacher, helping to build enthusiasm.

LEAD TEACHER

I. **Introduction:** Bang the jar of bubbles on the table, saying, *"Bubbles! Bubbles!"* If anyone has difficulty, say, *"Sit in chair, Maria."* Help the children physically if they need it.

II. **Step-by-step:**
1. Bang the jar down in front of each individual child, saying, *"Bubbles! Bubbles!"* Individualize the approach according to the child's level.
2. Allow one child to open the jar (he may need some help). Blow bubbles for the children, attempting to get their attention and saying, *"Blow!"*
3. Say excitedly, *"Bubbles! Bubbles!"* and blow them in each child's direction so he becomes aware of them.

4. Give each child a chance to blow bubbles. Say, *"Blow."* Encourage the children to touch the bubbles.

III. **Ending:** Blow some bubbles. Pop them, saying after each one has popped, *"Bye-bye bubbles."* After all of them have disappeared, say, *"Bubbles gone!"*

IV. **Suggestions:** You may blow air on the child's hand to show him what blow means. Then blow a bubble. Move the bubble wand close to the individual child so he can attempt to blow.

CSID Learning Experience/Hello Time

Developmental Therapy Objective C-8/to answer a child's and adult's questions or requests with recognizable, meaningful, relevant word(s)

Area: Communication *Stage:* II *Name:* Telephone Talk	*Cross-Reference Objectives:* Behavior 8–10 Communication 13 Socialization 13–14 Academics 18
Materials/Special Instructions Two play telephones or cardboard phones	*Support Teacher* Help individual children participate.

LEAD TEACHER

I. **Introduction:** Say, "*I hear a telephone ringing. Ring, ring!*" Get out the telephones and pretend to answer one saying, "*Yes, operator, it's hello time. Everyone is going to get a turn to say hello.*"

II. **Step-by-step:**
1. Explain that you're going to call Reginald. Then give him one telephone.
2. Say, "*Ring, ring!*" Encourage him to pick up the receiver if he hesitates at first. Then say, "*Hello, who is this?*" Wait for him to answer, and then identify yourself.
3. Ask simple questions like, "*How are you?*" or "*What colors are you wearing?*"
4. Say goodbye and then ask Reginald to give the phone to another child.
5. Repeat for the other children.

III. **Ending:** When talking to the last child, tell him Hello Time is almost over and mention something about the next activity. Ask for his phone and put both of them away.

IV. **Suggestions:** Have two children talk together so that one child calls another. Encourage them to ask each other simple questions. If the children need an additional model, direct the support teacher to answer the phone the first time and model the conversation with her.

CSID Learning Experience/Hello Time

Developmental Therapy Objective S-1/to be aware of others

Area: Socialization *Stage:* I *Name:* Ball Roll	*Cross-Reference Objectives* Behavior 0–4, 7 Communication 0–3 Socialization 2–4, 7 Academics 6, 7
Materials/Special Instructions Small rubber ball	*Support Teacher* Direct the children to the lead teacher, moving each child through the activity if needed. Make gestures for waving if the child has no verbal skills. Encourage the child to say *"Hi!"* or wave to another child. Give praise for attempts.

LEAD TEACHER

I. **Introduction:** Take the ball from the cabinet. Say, *"I have a ball!"*

II. **Step-by-step:**
1. *"Hi, Mike! Hi, Sue!"* Repeat, speaking to all the children at the table.
2. Then roll the ball to the first child and say (with animation), *"Hi, Mike!"*
3. Direct Mike, saying *"Roll ball to Sue,"* and help him roll the ball to her. Praise him for his best efforts.

III. **Ending:** Put the ball in the cabinet, saying, *"Time to stop! Ball is gone."*

IV. **Suggestions:** If a child has no verbal skills, encourage eye contact and then help him roll the ball back to you. Each child has a turn to roll the ball and say, *"Hi,"* to another. If the child throws the ball, give him the ball again and repeat, *"Roll ball."* If a child moves from the table, say, *"Mike wants ball? Sit in chair."* If the child does not sit in his chair after verbal cues and stimulus from the ball, the support teacher moves in and helps him sit down.

CSID Learning Experience/Hello Time

Developmental Therapy Objective S-11/to exhibit a beginning emergence of self

Area Socialization *Stage:* I *Name:* Mirror! Mirror!	*Cross-Reference Objectives:* Behavior 0–2, 4 Communication 0–3 Socialization 1, 2, 7 Academics 1, 2, 4, 8–9, 15
Materials/Special Instructions Make-up mirror(s). If the child avoids looking into the mirror, stand directly behind him. Hold his head so he will see himself in the mirror. If the child is frightened, do not persist. Let him touch the mirror lights and the mirror.	*Support Teacher* Work with individual children following the instructions for the lead teacher.

LEAD TEACHER

I. **Introduction:** Take the mirror from the cabinet, placing it in the center of the table. Then verbalize, *"Mirror! See mirror!"* Turn on the mirror lights and look into the mirror, exaggerating facial expressions. Say, *"Mirror, lights on."*

II. **Step-by-step:**
   1. Place the mirror in front of a child, gently directing the child's face to the mirror. If he looks momentarily at himself, praise the child, saying, *"Look at John!"*
   2. Point to the eyes in the mirror. *"See eyes!"* Repeat with nose, ears, and other body parts. Always verbalize each process.

   3. Give every child a chance with the mirror, following the same procedure. Encourage verbal children to say, *"Mirror,"* *"Lights,"* *"Eyes,"* *"Nose,"* etc.

III. **Ending:** Turn out the mirror lights, saying, *"Mirror, lights off."*

IV. **Suggestions:** Use a large mirror, laying it on the table. Or, use the observation window as a mirror. Take the children over to the window. Urge them to look at themselves or the other children.

CSID Learning Experience/Hello Time

Developmental Therapy Objective S-11/to exhibit a beginning emergence of self

Area: Socialization	*Cross-Reference Objectives:*
Stage: I	Behavior 0–4, 6–7
Name: Puppet Play	Communication 0–3
	Socialization 1–2, 4
	Academics 1–4

Materials/Special Instructions	*Support Teacher*
Hand puppets	Direct the children to the lead teacher. If a child gets up from his chair, verbally direct him back to it. If he does not respond to verbal direction, assist the child to the chair and then praise him for sitting down. "Good sitting!"

LEAD TEACHER

I. **Introduction:** Announce the activity and quickly take a puppet from the cabinet, putting it on your hand.

II. **Step-by-step:**
1. Say emphatically, "*It's Oscar!*" Then have the puppet look at each child and greet him. "*Hi, Joey!*" Wait for the child's response.
2. If the child cannot respond verbally, encourage a hand movement, maybe waving the puppet's arm or having the puppet touch the child.

3. If the child gives no motor response, take his hand and gently shape a response.

III. **Ending:** After the puppet has greeted all the children, say, "*Oscar's leaving.*" Then have the puppet wave and say, "*Bye-bye!*" to each child.

IV. **Suggestions:** Allow each child to have a turn with the puppet. Direct the child to say "*Hi*" to each of the other children at the table. Then have him give the puppet to one of the other children.

WORK TIME

CSID Learning Experience/Work Time

Developmental Therapy Objective A-4/to respond with motor and body responses to complex environmental and verbal stimuli

Area: Academics *Stage:* I *Name:* Chips in Slot	*Cross-Reference Objectives:* Behavior 1–4, 7, 10 Communication 1–2 Socialization 1–4, 7 Academics 1–3, 5–6, 10
Materials/Special Instructions Plastic poker chips and a container with a slot cut in the top (A coffee can with a plastic lid works well.)	*Support Teacher* Direct the child to look at the slot and put the chips in the container. Repeat the same verbal cues as the lead teacher and work with individual children who need help.

LEAD TEACHER

I. **Introduction:** Remove the container from the cabinet. Bang it on the table to get the child's attention if needed. Then take a poker chip and put it in the slot on the top of the container. Try to get the child's attention as you do so. Shake the container. Repeat the action exaggeratedly, saying, *"Put in!"*

II. **Step-by-step:**
1. Give the children containers and chips, directing each to put the chips in the container. *"Put in!"* For the child who is unable to begin the process, put a chip in his hand and move it to the slot. Then praise him. *"Joey put in!"*
2. Repeat the process.

III. **Ending:** After all the chips are in or the child tires, bang the container on the table, saying, *"Chips in! Joey put in chips."*

IV. **Suggestions:** Have the children who do not respond at all put the chips in the can without the top on it.

CSID Learning Experience/Work Time

Developmental Therapy Objective A-5/to respond with rudimentary fine and gross motor skills to simple manipulative tasks associated with the 24-month age level

Area: Academics *Stage:* I *Name:* Sponge and Water	*Cross-Reference Objectives:* Behavior 0–4 Communication 0–5 Socialization 1–2, 7 Academics 1–4
Materials/Special Instructions Large natural sponges and foil pie plates for each child, bowl of water, and box	**Support Teacher** Encourage the children to explore sponges by rubbing a sponge on their faces or arms. Assist the children in the squeezing of sponges if needed. Praise the children for attending and redirect those who are not.

LEAD TEACHER

I. **Introduction:** Shake the box containing the sponges and foil plates to motivate the children.

II. **Step-by-step:**
1. Reach into the box, compressing the sponge in your hand. Excitedly let it pop out of your hand onto table and say, "*Sponge!*" Repeat several times.
2. Allow each child to feel the sponge, rub it on his cheeks or arms, and squeeze it.
3. Then take the plates and noisily place one in front of each child, repeating, "*Plate!*" Dip the sponge into the bowl of water and squeeze some of the water onto each plate.
4. Give each child a sponge and assist him in putting it into the water and squeezing the water onto his plate. Constantly verbalize, "*Put sponge in water. Squeeze*

sponge." Encourage the use of the controlled vocabulary: *sponge, plate,* and *water* or approximations.

III. **Ending:** Announce that the activity is "*Almost over,*" giving each child one more opportunity to squeeze the sponge. Quickly collect the plates and pour the water from them into the bowl. Make a big production of pouring the water. Say, "*Water in bowl.*" Then collect the sponges, asking each child to "*Put sponge in box.*" Praise each child for correct response as well as any effort.

IV. **Suggestions:** Teacher must be alert and in control of the water. It is a tempting stimulus to some children, and they may be attracted to the bowl of water rather than the planned activity. Watch out for children wanting to pat their hands in the water. Redirect by getting them involved with the sponge.

CSID Learning Experience/Work Time

Developmental Therapy Objective A-11/to match similar objects with different attributes

Area: Academics	*Cross-Reference Objectives:*
Stage: I	Behavior 0–4
Name Form Box	Communication 1–2
	Socialization 1, 7
	Academics 1–5

Materials/Special Instructions	*Support Teacher*
A form box (box with different shaped slots and tokens designed to go into these slots)	Verbalize to each child, "*Put in. Look at circle.*" If a child drops material on the floor, direct him to "*Pick up,*" moving him through this if necessary. Praise the child for an appropriate response.

LEAD TEACHER

I. **Introduction:** Initially give the child a form box, with circles (discs) only. Demonstrate to the child by putting a square in the correct slot and then a circle, saying, "*Put in!*" or "*Put!*"

II. **Step-by-step:**
1. Put the form box in front of a child and take out the circles, verbalizing to him, "*Put in.*" If the child turns his head away, direct him to look at the circle and move his hand to the correct slot. Praise the child saying, "*Look! Joey put in!*"

2. Give the child another circle to put in the slot. Do not help him this time. See if he can complete the task without assistance. If the child does not, help him through again, continuing to praise him for working on the task.

III. **Ending:** When the child has put in all the circles, pick up the box and shake it, saying, "*Joey put in circles!*"

IV. **Suggestions:** If the box has many shaped holes, tape over the extra openings at first so the child more easily understands what you want him to do.

CSID Learning Experience/Work Time

Developmental Therapy Objective A-11/to match similar objects with different attributes

Area: Academics *Stage:* I *Name:* Puzzle Play	*Cross-Reference Objectives:* Behavior 7, 10 Communication 1–5 Socialization 4, 7, 15 Academics 4–7, 10

Materials/Special Instructions A puzzle for each child	*Support Teacher* Keep the child at the task with encouraging remarks. Help the individual child fit the pieces in the puzzle. Have higher level children name things in the puzzle and count the pieces. Inform the lead teacher when a child has finished his puzzle. Direct the child to the lead teacher for a new puzzle.

LEAD TEACHER

I. **Introduction:** *"It's puzzle time! Let's go sit in chairs. I have puzzles!"* Quickly take the puzzles from the cabinet. (To the table).

II. **Step-by-step:**
1. Give each child a puzzle. Have the child with verbal skills ask for the puzzle: *"I want puzzle."* Another child might be expected to make the /p/ sound, while a child just beginning to respond to materials might only be able to reach for the puzzle.
2. Have the child take out one puzzle piece at a time. Ask him to replace the piece; then another piece is removed and replaced.

3. For children with higher skills, several puzzle pieces are removed and replaced; then remove and replace all of the pieces.

III. **Ending:** When the child has finished the puzzle, say, *"Give me puzzle."* Assist the child in giving if necessary. *"The puzzle is done!"*

IV. **Suggestions:** Allow the child to manipulate the pieces for a few seconds. Then guide the child's hand or tell him, *"Turn,"* until the pieces fit. Praise the child for putting puzzle pieces in place: *"Good job"* or *"You put pieces in!"* If the children have withdrawn from the activity, bang the puzzle on the table or dump out the pieces loudly to attract their attention.

CSID Learning Experience/Work Time

Developmental Therapy Objective A-16/to perform fine motor coordination activities at the 3–4-year level

Area: Academics *Stage:* I *Name:* Cutting on Lines	*Cross-Reference Objectives:* Behavior 1, 2, 4, 10 Communication 1, 3–5, 7, 9 Socialization 1–4, 7 Academics 6
Materials/Special Instructions Four or five long strips of construction or manilla paper, two inches wide, divided by lines into segments of equal size	*Support Teacher* Follow the same instructions as for the lead teacher in working with the individual child.

LEAD TEACHER

I. **Introduction:** Say emphatically, *"Let's cut,"* and demonstrate by snipping off a piece of the paper.

II. **Step-by-step:**
1. Give the child a pair of scissors, having him use language if possible. For example, help the child repeat the phrase word by word, *"I want scissors,"* or ask, *"What do you want?"* Expected response, *"Scissors."*
2. For the child who has not learned to cut, it will be necessary to guide his hand or use special scissors. Illustrate for him, showing how to cut on lines. Help the child focus on the lines. Use such verbalizations as, *"Open . . . close."*
3. After the child has snipped all the paper or shows signs of tiring, ask for the scissors. Provide a sheet of colored construction paper and paste. Show the child how to paste out segments on paper. *"Paste paper."* Show enthusiasm for results.

III. **Ending:** Admire the child's work. Assist the child in displaying it on a bulletin board or other appropriate place.

IV. **Suggestions:** When the child masters cutting straight lines, use the same approach for cutting curved lines, half circles, complete circles, squares, and then other shapes.

CSID Learning Experience/Work Time

Developmental Therapy Objective A-16/to perform fine motor coordination activities at the 3–4-year level

Area: Academics *Stage:* I *Name:* Stringing Beads	***Cross-Reference Objectives:*** Behavior 4, 9–10 Communication 1–3, 8–9 Socialization 2, 4, 7, 9 Academics 8, 10–11, 15
Materials/Special Instructions Colored beads, string, and container for beads	***Support Teacher*** Work with the other half of the children on different types of individualized work. Follow the lead teacher's instructions when helping a child with beads.

LEAD TEACHER

I. **Introduction:** String several beads, holding the string high so the children see the beads fall. Say, "*I'm stringing beads.*"

II. **Step-by-step:**
1. Show the child the beads and ask, "*Do you want beads?*" If the child is able, wait for him to ask or sign for them.
2. Repeat the preceding step with the string.
3. Say, "*Put on bead.*" Give the child as much help as he needs.
4. Repeat for several beads.

III. **Ending:** Instruct the child to look at the beads. After the child has strung all the beads, have him count them or you do it as he watches. The beads can then be tied, putting them around the child's neck. "*Pretty! Beads!*"

IV. **Suggestions:** Once the children master stringing, the beads can be used to help teach colors. Do not, however, attempt to do both simultaneously if both tasks are new to the child.

CSID Learning Experience/Work Time

Developmental Therapy Objective A-17/to recognize several colors

Area: Academics *Stage:* I *Name:* Color in Cartons	*Cross-Reference Objectives:* Behavior 1–4, 10 Communication 2–3, 8–9 Socialization 4, 7–8, 10–11 Academics 6, 10–12
Materials/Special Instructions Small objects (cardboard disks or little blocks) colored red, blue, or yellow (with a nontoxic substance) and three pint-size milk cartons covered respectively with red, blue, and yellow construction paper	*Support Teacher* Direct the child to the lead teacher. Give support to the child. Physically assist the child in sorting if the child is unable to do it alone. Pull back to see if the child will continue on his own.

LEAD TEACHER

I. **Introduction:** Lead the children over to the table. Give each child a box containing the different colored objects. Then give each child the colored milk cartons. Point to each carton and say distinctly, *"Red, blue, yellow."*

II. **Step-by-step:**
1. Instruct the child to put all the red objects in the red carton, all blue in the blue carton, etc.
2. Demonstrate for the children if necessary. For children who are just beginning to learn these basic colors, go through the activity by putting the child's hand on each color repeating, *"This is red, this is blue, this is yellow."* If a child puts an object in the wrong color carton, remove the object and direct the child to look at it. Then point to the correct carton.

III. **Ending:** Ask the child to give you the cartons, saying, *"Give me red,"* *"Give me blue,"* etc. Point to the correct carton if necessary.

IV. **Suggestions:** Have the child repeat the color names. After he puts an object in a container, ask, *"What color is it?"* Model, saying, *"It is red."* When the child has mastered these three colors, add three more. Then do all six together.

CSID Learning Experience/Work Time

Developmental Therapy Objective A-17/to recognize several colors

Area: Academics *Stage:* I *Name:* Colored Pegs	*Cross-Reference Objectives:* Behavior 4, 8, 10–11 Communication 2–8, 11–12 Socialization 3, 7–10, 13–14, 16–18 Academics 4, 7–9, 14–16, 20–21, 30

Materials/Special Instructions Large peg board with colored pegs	*Support Teacher* Direct the child to the lead teacher for instructions. If the child is reluctant to put the peg in the board, make a game of it by exaggerating hand movements in putting peg in holes. If the child still resists, take his hand and move it to the peg board. *"Reginald put peg in! Good boy!"* If the child picks up the wrong one when asked to give a certain color, repeat, *"Give me red. This is blue."* Point to the red peg, repeating, *"This is red!"*

LEAD TEACHER

I. **Introduction:** Take the peg board from the cabinet, saying, *"I have peg board. See holes?"* Point to the holes. Then pick up a container of assorted colored pegs.

II. **Step-by-step:**
1. Hold up the red peg and say, *"Here is red peg! Pick up red peg. Put in red peg."* Ask the children, *"What color is it?"* Wait for a response from verbal children. Nonverbal children can indicate color by pointing or picking up peg.
2. After the verbal child can name red consistently, hold up red and yellow pegs and say, *"Here is red peg and here is yellow peg."* Then repeat sequence as outlined in the first step.
3. Continue pairing pegs of two different colors (one known and one unknown).

III. **Ending:** Ask the child to put all the red pegs in the container, then all the blue pegs, etc. Continue until all the pegs have been put away.

IV. **Suggestions:** For the child who is just beginning to learn colors, use only one color of pegs. Make a square design with the pegs, saying, *"I'm making a square. Maria, make a square!"* Give help as needed. After all the pegs are on the board, give instructions, such as, *"Sue, give me all the red pegs"* or *"Show me an orange peg."* Constantly praise the child for appropriate responses.

CSID Learning Experience/Work Time

Developmental Therapy Objective A-26/to categorize simple pictures that are different but have generally similar characteristics or associations

Area: Academics *Stage:* II *Name:* Picture Match	*Cross-Reference Objectives:* Behavior 10, 12 Communication 8–9, 11 Socialization 14 Academics 25

Materials/Special Instructions Sets of similar pictures (DLM cards or pictures from magazines) pasted on 3″ × 5″ cards or paper. Use commonplace things such as pictures of shoes and socks, tables, chairs, food, etc.	*Support Teacher* Direct the child to the pictures or objects to praise him for good work. If the child puts a wrong card in the pile, pick up the card, saying, "*This is a chair. Chairs go here.*" Keep the other children interested while they wait for their turns.

LEAD TEACHER

I. **Introduction:** Say excitedly, "*Let's sit in the chairs and look at pictures!*"

II. **Step-by-step:**
1. Take a set of four or five cards with pictures of tables on them and another set of cards with pictures of chairs. Make sure the tables and chairs are of different styles.
2. Hold a card in front of the child, verbalizing, "*This is a table.*" Go through all the pictures of the tables, showing each and placing them in one pile.
3. Then take the pictures of the chairs and place them in another pile, showing the child each picture and verbalizing, "*This is a chair*" or "*Chair.*"
4. Next say, "*I put all the tables here and all the chairs here,*" pointing to each pile.
5. Then take the cards, mix them together, and instruct the child to put all the chairs together and all the tables together.

III. **Ending:** When the child has separated the tables and chairs, collect the cards and say, "*All tables together. All chairs together. Let's stop! Put away.*"

IV. **Suggestions:** If a child takes the cards and does not discriminate or looks at you questioningly, take the cards and ask, "*What is this?*" Help the child respond, "*Chair.*" Take a picture of a table and ask the child to identify that. Place the picture of each in front of the child, side by side. Then hold up the cards for the child to see and say, "*Find a chair.*" When the child takes a card, instruct him to put it with the other picture of a chair. Follow the same process through all cards and then reflect to the child, "*Good! You put the chairs together and the tables together,*" pointing to each set. Repeat the activity if the child has not become restless. For use with symbols, the word "chair" may be written on a piece of paper and the word "table" on another piece of paper. Place the words in front of the child, pointing to each word. Have him say the words with you, pointing to each one. Then instruct the child to put together the cards with the appropriate words. After a child has mastered one set of pictures, then a new set is introduced. Each one is a little more complex.

CSID Learning Experience/Exercise Time

Developmental Therapy Objective B-9/to wait without physical intervention by adult

Area: Behavior *Stage:* II *Name:* Obstacle Course	*Cross-Reference Objectives:* Behavior 4, 8, 11–12 Communication 3–5, 7, 12 Socialization 3, 6–8, 10, 13–14 Academics 13, 28
Materials/Special Instructions Large plastic circle and triangle such as those used for sides of snap wall cubes and a big ball or punching bag for additional stimulus	*Support Teacher* Keep the remaining children attending to the child crawling through triangle. A child may be having a hard time waiting. You might say, *"It's Mike's turn now. Then Joey will have a turn."* For children who are waiting, *"I like the way Sue and Joey are waiting for their turns."*

LEAD TEACHER

I. **Introduction:** Announce the activity and direct the children to sit in the exercise area. Set up the course by placing the triangle, the circle, and the ball so that they face the child.

II. **Step-by-step:**
1. Verbalize dramatically, *"We are going to crawl through the triangle,"* (touching the triangle). *"Then crawl through the circle"* (pointing to the circle). *"Next, hit the ball."*
2. Observe the group and ask, *"Who wants a turn?"* Let a child go first whom you feel understands the directions best. Or, call on a child who is having a hard time waiting. Verbalize to each child at his turn, *"Crawl through the triangle. Crawl through the circle. Now hit the ball."* Each child is given a turn or several turns.

III. **Ending:** Announce that the activity is almost over and let each child have a last turn. *"Last turn for Sue! Last turn for Maria!"* If child lingers in triangle, encourage him to come through and hit the ball, or say, *"Hurry, Joey wants a turn."*

IV. **Suggestions:** To make the activity more exciting count to 10 during each child's turn. The child has to be back to his seat before you finish. Waiting children can count too.

CSID Learning Experience/Exercise Time

Developmental Therapy Objective B-11/to participate in movement activities such as play time, mat time, games, music, and art time activities without physical intervention by adult

Area: Socialization *Stage:* II *Name:* Happy Moving	*Cross-Reference Objectives:* Behavior 12 Communication 9–11 Socialization 13, 15, 18 Academics 28–29
Materials/Special Instructions Teacher must prepare verse endings in advance.	*Support Teacher* Assist the children in sitting in a circle. Begin imitating the actions of the lead teacher to provide a model for the children. Direct the children to the lead teacher as you encourage them to participate.

LEAD TEACHER

I. **Introduction:** Begin singing, *"If you're happy and you know it,"* as you seat the children in a circle on the floor.

II. **Step-by-step:**
1. Sing the song and act out the motions with much animation.
2. Help the children attend to the motions. Then have the children imitate the actions. The success of this will depend upon your pacing each verse to maintain interest.
3. Determine in advance endings to each verse that the children will understand and enjoy. *"If you're happy and you know it, clap your hands,"* or *"Wear a smile,"* or *"Turn your head."* These three motions are common and fun for most Stage Two children.

III. **Ending:** For a final verse to prepare for the next activity, sing, *"If you're happy and you know it, sit right down,"* modeling for the child where to sit.

IV. **Suggestions:** For other verses you could ask the children to touch their toes, feet, heads, or other body parts or substitute *"Stand up, jump,"* or any other developmental sequence to be worked on. Encourage each child to suggest a motion.

CSID Learning Experience/Exercise Time

Developmental Therapy Objective S-17/to participate in cooperative activities or projects with another child during playtime, indoor or outdoor

Area: Socialization *Stage:* II *Name:* Rope Pull	*Cross-Reference Objectives:* Behavior 11 Communication 6 Socialization 13 Academics 5, 6
Materials/Special Instructions Rope	*Support Teacher* See **Suggestions.**

LEAD TEACHER

I. **Introduction:** Take the rope off the shelf, saying with enthusiasm, *"I have a rope."*

II. **Step-by-step:**
1. Make a line on the floor with masking tape and place half of the children on one side of the line with the support teacher. Take charge of the other half.
2. Direct the children to pick up the rope and pull, trying to pull one group across the line.
3. Excitedly encourage each child to say, *"Pull!"*

III. **Ending:** Return the rope to the shelf, saying, *"Pulling is over!"*

IV. **Suggestions:** With the support teacher, hold the rope and have the children step over it. Raise the rope and have the children go under it. If the children are not able to handle directions, move them through the activity and have each child alternate holding the rope with the support teacher. Concentrate on the words *over* and *under*. Have the support teacher and the child swing the rope while you help another child jump over it.

CSID Learning Experience/Exercise Time

Developmental Therapy Objective A-4/to respond with motor and body responses to complex environmental and verbal stimuli

Area: Academics
Stage: I
Name: Basic Exercises

Cross-Reference Objectives:
Behavior   1–3
Communication   1, 2
Socialization   1–4, 6–7
Academics   6

Materials/Special Instructions
None

Support Teacher
Assist the lead teacher by moving the children through the activity as much as is needed, praising any attempts to imitate movements.

LEAD TEACHER

I. **Introduction:** *"It's exercise time. Let's go sit on floor."* Have the children go to the appropriate area and sit down. Help the children who need assistance through any activity.

II. **Step-by-step:**
  1. Have the children lie on the floor on their backs. *"Let's lie down."* Demonstrate for them.
  2. Next have the children sit up, then lie back down, repeating several times, *"Up and down! Up and down!"*

III. **Ending:** Announce, *"Exercise time is over!"*

IV. **Suggestions:** If there are several who are not able to follow the instructions, sit close to half of the children and have the support teacher sit close to the other half, moving them up and down. Holding each child's arm, gently pull him up and then push him down to a supine position. After doing the sit up, say, *"Now let's put legs up; now, down!"* using the same technique stated above. If a child is frightened by these exercises, you might have him roll on the floor or simply raise alternate arms while lying on the floor.

CSID Learning Experience/Exercise Time

Developmental Therapy Objective A-13/to perform body coordination activities at the 3–4-year level

Area: Academics
Stage: I
Name: Board Walk

Cross-Reference Objectives:
Behavior   0–4
Communication   1
Socialization   1–3, 6–7
Academics   1–2, 4

Materials/Special Instructions
Board 1″ × 1′ × 6′

Support Teacher
Follow up the group to be sure everyone gets over to the exercise area while the lead teacher goes ahead and sits with the children who are ready first. When the lead teacher gets up, help the children stay seated either by touch or by saying "*Sit!*" Point to the lead teacher and say, "*Look!,*" if a child is not attending to the lead. When a child finishes his turn on the board, welcome him back and help him sit while the lead teacher gets another child up to walk. If a child starts to lie down, help him sit up, perhaps in your lap; help him to attend. Constantly watch each child, and keep him attending by touching or using verbal support such as "*Mike, look!*"

LEAD TEACHER

I. **Introduction:** Lead children to the exercise area and sit down. After everyone is seated (help children sit down only if they need this), jump up, quickly get board from corner, and noisily place it on the floor.

II. **Step-by-step:**
1. Walk very deliberately with exaggerated movements on the board. Verbalize slowly and expressively, "*Walk, walk, walk!*" Then jump off the end of the board, making a noise.
2. Announce, "*It's Mike's turn to walk on the board. Mike, let's walk.*" Physically help the child to get up if he doesn't move. Then help him step onto the board, holding his hand to help him complete the

task. After he finishes, reinforce with whatever is meaningful for him (touching, hugging, handshake), and say, "*Good! You walked on board.*"
3. Help each child walk on the board.

III. **Ending:** Return the board to corner, saying, "*Walking on board is over.*"

IV. **Suggestions:** When developmental level permits, use a thicker board of narrower width. For children working on A-13, the board should remain flat on the floor. This same board can be introduced again with a slight elevation from the floor for A-29, a Stage Two objective for refining balance and large muscle coordination.

CSID Learning Experience/Exercise Time

Developmental Therapy Objective A-29/to perform body coordination at the five-year level

Area: Academics *Stage:* II *Name:* Board Walk	*Cross-Reference Objectives:* Behavior 1–5, 7, 9, 10–12 Communication 1–3 Socialization 1–4, 6–7, 14 Academics 2, 4, 6, 13, 17

Materials/Special Instructions Walking rail or 6–8-foot board 4 inches wide. For lower level children it is important to make the activity very arousing. Therefore, the teacher should make quick and dramatic movements to direct the children's attention to the designated area for the activity.	*Support Teacher* Go to the designated area, encouraging the children to follow. Assist the children in removing their shoes and socks when necessary. Encourage the children to attend to the lead teacher and each other during the activity. Verbalize to them when appropriate concerning the activity.

LEAD TEACHER

I. **Introduction:** *"It's exercise time!"* Begin by taking off your own shoes, reflecting, *"We are going to take off our shoes and socks."* Then encourage children to take off their shoes and socks. (This could be a good motivator for a child who is reluctant to come over to the area.)

II. **Step-by-step:**
1. Take out the board, drop it on the floor noisily, and walk on it deliberately. *"W-a-l-k, walk, walk."* When you reach the end of the board, jump off dramatically.
2. Take each child one at a time for a walk on the board. The support teacher works with the others.
3. For poorly coordinated children, walk closely behind the child, guiding his feet on the board. It is important for the child to be barefoot in order to get the feel of the board.
4. If the child is unable to jump off the board when he reaches the end, physically jump him off, making sounds of pleasure.

III. **Ending:** Announce, *"Walking on board is almost over. Let's put on our shoes!"* Touch the shoes and socks, holding up the socks. Assist the children as necessary, encouraging them to dress themselves.

IV. **Suggestions:** During this exercise while the children are barefoot, a good opportunity is provided to explore feet and toes by having the children touch their feet, wiggle their toes, or touch the teacher's or another child's toes.

YUM-YUM TIME

CSID Learning Experience/Yum-Yum Time

Developmental Therapy Objective C-2/to respond to verbal stimulus with a motor behavior C-3/to respond to verbal stimulus and single object with a recognizable approximation of the appropriate verbal response

Area: Communication *Stage:* I *Name:* Apple Slice	*Cross-Reference Objectives:* Behavior 1–4 Communication 1, 4–5 Socialization 1–4 Academics 6, 8
Materials/Special Instructions Shiny red apples and a table knife	*Support Teacher* Help the children back to table. Direct the children to the lead teacher. Use the same verbalizations she uses to keep individual children attending.

LEAD TEACHER

I. **Introduction:** *"It's yum-yum time! Let's go sit in chairs."* Hold up the apple saying, *"It's an apple!"*

II. **Step-by-step:**
1. Frequently say, *"Apple,"* allowing each child to feel it.
2. Make an elaborate production of slicing the apple into tiny slices.
3. Offer each child a slice, holding it in your hand until he responds with whatever language he is able to produce. For one child, just having him taste it is the objective. For another, any verbal response is acceptable.
4. Give each child a small piece every time he responds. Say, *"Good apple!"* You may ask the children the color of the apple, explore the seeds, talk about the sound made in chewing, etc.

III. **Ending:** Announce, *"Yum-Yum Time is almost over. I have more apple. Who wants apple?"* Wait for the child's response. Then give a slice of apple to him as he indicates he wants more. When only one piece of apple remains, explain, *"Apple is almost gone."* When the last piece of apple is given, exclaim dramatically, *"Apple is all gone."*

IV. **Suggestions:** Offer a piece of the apple to children who will not eat, placing it in front of them. Bite a slice of apple saying, *"Good apple!,"* and try to entice the child to take a bite. If a child knocks or throws the piece of apple on the floor, have him pick it up. Then remove the apple, saying, *"Marie doesn't like apple."* Use this same format for other visually stimulating foods.

CSID Learning Experience/Yum-Yum Time

Developmental Therapy Objective C-5/to produce recognizable single words

Area: Communication
Stage: I
Name: Chip Talk

Cross-Reference Objectives:
Behavior   0–2, 4–5
Communication   0–1, 3–4
Socialization   0–2
Academics   1–4

Materials/Special Instructions
The main variation here is the type of food. It *must* be motivating for the child. Use fruit pieces, crackers, gelatin blocks (mix 2–3 envelopes of plain gelatin with one large box of flavored gelatin; Mix with 3–4 cups of boiling water and refrigerate until hard), pickles, doughnut pieces, bits of cheese, marshmallows, raw vegetable pieces, potato or corn chips, popcorn, etc.

Support Teacher
Repeat particular sounds to the children whom lead teacher is not involved with. Work on helping to elicit speech.

LEAD TEACHER

I. **Introduction:** *"Now it's yum-yum time."* Excitedly produce the food. Shake the container to get the children interested.

II. **Step-by-step:**
1. Place the food, chips for instance, at the child's level.
2. Accentuate the beginning sound of the food, *"Ch, ch, ch- ip,"* in a child's face.
3. If he doesn't respond, place his hand on your mouth, repeat, *"Ch, ch, ch- ip,"* and then put his hand on his mouth, constantly saying *"Ch-ch-ch-ip."*

4. If the child makes the sound (or even if he only approximates it), immediately give the chip to him.

III. **Ending:** After each child has had a chance to eat, remove the food and say, *"Sue ate chip, Joey ate chip,"* etc.

IV. **Suggestions:** Talk to the parents and the other teachers about particular foods each child might enjoy. Urge them to help by expecting some language from the children on a consistent basis.

STORY TIME

CSID Learning Experience/Story Time

Developmental Therapy Objective C-0/to produce sounds

Area: Communication *Stage:* I *Name:* Puppet Sound	*Cross-Reference Objectives:* Behavior 0–3 Communication 1–5 Socialization 1–4 Academics 1–3

Materials/Special Instructions
A special box of hand puppets which evoke interest from the children and can elicit the sound you are working on. For example, if you are working on /s/, use a snake puppet.

Support Teacher
Repeat whatever the lead teacher says to each child. Aid the lead teacher in stimulating each child in the group. For instance, a child may need assistance in following the lead teacher's command.

LEAD TEACHER

I. **Introduction:** Put the puppet on your hand and make the "*s-s-s*" sound. Show each child the snake puppet while continually saying, "*S-s-s-snake!*"

II. **Step-by-step:**
1. Encourage each child to make the snake's sound.
2. If a child is not attending, have the puppet kiss the child, or put it directly in front of his face. Take the child's hand and verbalize the "*s-s-s*" on his hand so he can feel it. It may even stimulate him more if you put the puppet on his hand and let him talk for it. This would make it more meaningful to him. If you have not heard the child say this particular sound, accept any sound he makes!
3. Return the puppet to the box and repeat Steps 1 and 2 with other puppets.

III. **Ending:** Announce that the activity is almost over and bring out each puppet to quickly review the sounds with the children. Return the puppets to the box.

IV. **Suggestions:** To generate interest, use puppets like the Cookie Monster puppet, which can be "fed" by the children through the hole in its mouth.

CSID Learning Experience/Story Time

Developmental Therapy Objective C-2/to respond to verbal stimulus with a motor behavior

Area: Communication *Stage:* I *Name:* Hand Puppets	*Cross-Reference Objectives:* Behavior 0–3 Communication 1, 3–5 Socialization 1–4 Academics 1–4, 6–10
Materials/Special Instructions Hand puppets in a bag	*Support Teacher* Help the children stay in control by directing them to look at the puppet. Make barking or other animal sounds as appropriate. Gently pat children who withdraw or seem afraid.

LEAD TEACHER

I. **Introduction:** *"It's story time! Let's go sit on floor."* When the children are seated, say, *"Let's see what's in this bag,"* and remove one of the puppets. *"It's a dog!"*

II. **Step-by-step:**
1. Interest the child in the dog puppet by making a barking sound. *"Woof! Woof!"*
2. Tickle each child with the puppet and have the child touch its mouth, ears, nose, etc. (depending upon level of development).
3. If the child is afraid of the puppet, gently pat it saying, *"Nice dog."*
4. When the child is ready, allow him to put his hand in the puppet and control it.
5. Give each child a turn. Then put the puppet back in the bag and take out another one.

III. **Ending:** When each child has had a turn with several puppets, return the puppets to the bag (have the children do this if possible) and say, *"Bye-bye dog. Bye-bye cat."*

IV. **Suggestions:** Use stuffed dogs and have the children touch and cuddle them. Gently pat dog, saying, *"Nice dog."* Encourage each child to touch the dog. *"Nice dog."*

CSID Learning Experience/Story Time

Developmental Therapy Objective C-8/to answer a child's and adult's questions or requests with recognizable, meaningful, relevant word(s)

Area: Communications *Stage:* II *Name:* Food Pictures	*Cross-Reference Objectives:* Behavior 9, 10 Communication 5, 9 Socialization 13, 14 Academics 12
Materials/Special Instructions Bright colorful pictures of favorite foods cut out of magazines and pasted on cardboard	*Support Teacher* Direct the child to the lead teacher. When the lead teacher asks for a certain picture and the child with that picture is not attending, direct him to it, saying, *"Joey has the orange."*

LEAD TEACHER

I. **Introduction:** *"It's story time. Let's go sit on the floor."* Display picture cards of different foods that might interest the children. Verbalize, "I have hamburger!" Rub your stomach, saying *"Mm—hamburger,"* while pretending to pick up hamburger and chew. Encourage each child to pretend to eat. *"Mm—hamburger!"* Then switch to another yummy picture and repeat with each card.

II. **Step-by-step:**
1. Hold up a picture of a hamburger and ask, *"What is this?"* Verbal children are expected to reply or repeat the word after you say it. Repeat for each picture, encouraging some verbal response from each child.
2. Give each child one picture as you name it.
3. Then ask, *"Who has the orange?"* The child with the orange holds that card up.

4. Ask for another card until all children have shown their pictures.

III. **Ending:** Collect cards. As you take each child's card, make eating sounds and say, *"Joey had the orange! Sue had the hamburger!"* etc.

IV. **Suggestions:** Give each child two pictures and ask him for a certain one so that he can discriminate between the two, or hold up a picture of ice cream, saying, *"Who likes ice cream?"* Support teacher enthusiastically says, *"I like ice cream!,"* as a model for the children. Encourage each child to respond with, *"I like ice cream."* If the child obviously dislikes a certain food, help him verbalize *"I don't like ice cream"* or perhaps just *"Yuk"* if that's all he can say.

CSID Learning Experience/Story Time

Developmental Therapy Objective A-7/to respond by simple discrimination of objects

Area: Academics *Stage:* I *Name:* Picking Fruits	*Cross-Reference Objectives:* Behavior 2, 3, 9, 10, 12 Communication 1–5 Socialization 2, 6–10, 14 Academics 2–4, 6, 8–11, 14

Materials/Special Instructions Plastic fruit or real fruit in a bag	*Support Teacher* Direct the children to the lead teacher. Encourage the child to attempt saying the words. If a child does not respond to the command from the lead teacher (*"Give me apple"*), take the child's hand and place on the apple, repeating, *"A-p-p-l-e!"*

LEAD TEACHER

I. **Introduction:** *"It's story time. Let's go sit on floor!"* Hold up in quick succession the plastic or real fruit. Say excitedly, *"Mm—apple! Mm—orange!"* etc., and make eating sounds.

II. **Step-by-step:**
1. Take one fruit and say to children, *"Look! It's an apple!"*
2. Then have children with verbal skills say, *"Apple."* Go on to another fruit and slowly repeat the name of each one, placing all of them on the floor.
3. Say, *"Maria, give me apple!"* Praise the child. *"Good! Maria gave me a apple."*
4. Then place the second fruit on the floor, name it, and continue, giving each child a turn to pick up one of the two fruits.

III. **Ending:** When all the fruit has been picked up, put it away, saying, *"Time to stop! Apple gone, orange gone,"* etc.

IV. **Suggestions:** The number of fruits may be increased to three or four. Objects may be changed to toys, cooking utensils, simple pictures, or geometric shapes, depending on the level of the children.

If a child picks up an orange instead of an apple, say, *"This is orange. Give me apple,"* and point to apple. Hopefully child will be able to respond correctly. Then praise her. *"Good! Maria gave me apple!"* Place another fruit on the floor and continue.

To vary the learning experience, put the plastic or real fruit in a paper bag. Show the children pictures of the fruit. Then take the bag and shake it excitedly, saying, *"What's in bag?"* Pass bag around to each child allowing him to remove one piece of fruit. Verbalize what each child has. Encourage the child to exchange his object with another child after eliciting verbalization and giving praise.

CSID Learning Experience/Story Time

Developmental Therapy Objective A-10/to demonstrate short term memory for sound patterns, objects, or people

Area: Academics *Stage:* I *Name:* Lost and Found	*Cross-Reference Objectives:* Behavior 0–3, 6 Communication 0–6 Socialization 2–4, 7 Academics 1–2, 6–9
Materials/Special Instructions Stuffed animals in a bag (one for each child in the group) and a towel. Carpet squares may be used to sit on. If they are used, have each child's name on a square.	**Support Teacher** Assist the children in getting to their places on the floor, directing them to the lead teacher and to the activity. *"Look, Joey. See dog?"* Praise the child for any appropriate response; redirect the child to what is happening if he is not attending.

LEAD TEACHER

I. **Introduction:** Announce the activity by saying excitedly, *"It's story time. Let's sit on floor."* Move to the area for Story Time. If carpet squares are used, place each square, saying the child's name as you place his square. Show the children the bag. *"Look! What is this?"*

II. **Step-by-step:**
1. Take the stuffed animals out of the bag, one at a time. *"I have a dog. What does dog say?"* Wait for each child's response and help him if he needs urging. *"Right! Dog says, woof! woof!"*

2. Say, *"I am going to hide dog."* Place the dog on the floor, put a towel over it, and say, *"Joey, find dog!"* Praise the child by responding, *"Joey found dog!"* Allow the child to keep the animal.

3. Give each child a chance to find an animal under the towel.

III. **Ending:** Announce that the activity is almost over and ask each child to return his animal to the bag, saying, *"Put dog in bag."*

IV. **Suggestions:** Use different objects in which the children have shown an interest, e.g., balls, trucks, and dolls.

CSID Learning Experience/Story Time

Developmental Therapy Objective A-19/to recognize detail in pictures by gesture or word

Area: Academics *Stage:* II *Name:* Action Pictures	*Cross-Reference Objectives:* Behavior 2, 4, 9–10, 12 Communication 2, 8–9, 12 Socialization 2–4, 7, 14 Academics 2, 4, 6

Materials/Special Instructions Simple picture cards or pictures from magazines pasted on construction paper. Use these pictures to elicit spontaneous or prompted speech. Have the children sit on floor in semicircle facing the teacher. For children who do not stay seated, using a corner of the room for story time is helpful. Be sure to use pictures that interest the children. They must be motivating or the activity won't work.	*Support Teacher* Assist the children to the area for Story Time and direct them to the teacher and picture while the lead teacher is working with another child. Nurture and praise by gently patting the child on the back or leg. If a child is having a hard time sitting, move next to him or put him on your lap.

LEAD TEACHER

I. **Introduction:** Occasionally pause to see if a child can name the activity first. Direct the children to the area for story time.

II. **Step-by-step:**
1. As soon as the children are seated, hold up a picture of a woman putting a cake in an oven and a boy with a mixing bowl (or something similar).
2. Say, "*Look!*" and point to the woman. "*Here are Mama (Mother) and John.*"
3. "*Joey, who is this?*" Joey, hopefully, will reply, "*Mama.*"
4. Then continue with, "*They are making cake!*" Ask another child, "*What are they doing?*" and repeat for

him, "*Making cake. Mike, say making cake!*" Take another picture and use the same techniques.

III. **Ending:** Announce that the activity is almost over, put the cards behind your back, and make believe with the children that you give each child a slice of cake. Pantomime slicing, passing, and eating. "*We can have cake again tomorrow.*"

IV. **Suggestions:** Ask the children to point to the stove or other objects in the picture. It may be necessary to put the pictures close to the children's faces to get their attention.

DANCE TIME

CSID Learning Experience/Dance Time

Developmental Therapy Objective B-11/to participate in movement activities such as play time, mat time, games, music, and art time activities without physical intervention by adult

Area: Behavior	**Cross-Reference Objectives:**
Stage: II	Behavior 2–4, 12
Name: Basic Movement	Communication 2
	Socialization 2–4, 6–7, 13, 15
	Academics 2–4, 6, 13

Materials/Special Instructions	*Support Teacher*
Record and record player or tape player. It is usually better to repeat the same record or alternate two selections so that the children can become familiar with the melodies.	Follow the lead teacher's directions and example with individual children. Reflect to them as they are dancing. Provide a model for the children who might not participate.

LEAD TEACHER

I. **Introduction:** *"Now it's dance time! Let's stand up."* Direct the children over to the appropriate area. Have the support teacher operate the record player. You may have one child help if this has been done before. If not, you may have one child (or more) who could learn this activity and would enjoy the process.

II. **Step-by-step:**
1. Say to the children, *"Let's dance!"*
2. Then begin the movements yourself, swaying and kicking smoothly and evenly. Show how much fun it is by your expression and verbalizations.
3. Try to get each child to respond. If you have to move some of the children physically, let the support teacher work with half of them.
4. Move one child near another to dance together. Join their hands and gently rock them to and fro with the music, reflecting, *"Reginald and Sue are dancing."* If a child pulls away, gently embrace him and continue dancing. This should be a very brief activity. Increase the time gradually as the children begin to enjoy the movements.

III. **Ending:** Announce the activity is almost over. Then shut off the record player and say, *"Stop! Dance time is over."*

IV. **Suggestions:** Keep the movements very simple, just a rocking from one foot to the other initially. The idea, as always, is to have the child first respond and then respond with pleasure. Begin with a child in each arm as you kneel on the floor, swaying back and forth gently. You may do only this for several activity periods before attempting to put two children together.

CSID Learning Experience/Dance Time

Developmental Therapy Objective B-11/to participate in movement activities such as play time, mat time, games, music, and art time activities without physical intervention by adult

Area: Behavior *Stage:* II *Name:* Musical Chairs	*Cross-Reference Objectives:* Behavior 4, 7, 12 Communication 2 Socialization 12–13, 15 Academics 4, 6, 13, 29

Materials/Special Instructions Record player, instrumental record, and chairs for each child and teacher	*Support Teacher* Assist children in taking their chairs over to the activity area. Operate the record player and join in the activity with the children when necessary, walking or dancing around chairs.

LEAD TEACHER

I. **Introduction:** Announce the activity. Then take your chair and encourage the children to bring their chairs. Line them up in the center of the floor.

II. **Step-by-step:**
1. When children are seated, dramatically instruct them to listen for the music. *"When the music starts we are going to dance around the chairs. When the music stops, we are going to sit down. N-o-w l-i-s-t-e-n!"*
2. Support teacher starts the record. Get up immediately, calling to the children, *"Come on! Let's dance!"* Make exaggerated movements to get the children involved. Take a child's hand if he continues to sit when the music starts.

3. Support teacher stops record. *"The music has stopped, let's sit down."*
4. Make sure all the children are seated before the record is started again.

III. **Ending:** Announce the activity is almost over and have everyone sit down one last time as the music stops.

IV. **Suggestions:** Some children will try to keep their own chair by sitting in it each time. Say, *"Now we can sit in any chair."* If child cannot accept this, say, *"Joey likes to sit in his chair. Maria can sit here."* Encourage each child to hold another's hand as they dance around the chairs.

OUTSIDE TIME

CSID Learning Experience/Outside Time

Developmental Therapy Objective B-6/to respond independently to several play materials

Area: Behavior
Stage: I
Name: Play Equipment

Cross-Reference Objectives:
Behavior   0–4, 7–8
Communication   1–4
Socialization   4, 13
Academics   1–4

Materials/Special Instructions
Appropriate toys for this stage are a big ball, a slide, a jungle gym, a swing, etc. Other activities may be adapted for Outside Time, including those for Play Time, Exercise Time, and Sand Time. The following learning experience describes how to approach and follow through with an outside activity.

Support Teacher
The object in this activity is to have every child involved in some form of play. The support teacher follows the same procedures as given for the lead teacher in helping individual children.

LEAD TEACHER

I. **Introduction:** *"It's outside time! Let's go play outside!"* Lead the children out of the building and toward the play area.

II. **Step-by-step:**
    1. *"Maria, let's slide!"* Encourage the child to climb the slide, saying, *"Up! Up!"* Help her if she needs it.
    2. After she is up, encourage her to come down by holding out your arms at the bottom of the slide. Say, *"Whee . . . down,"* expressing your excitement as she slides down.
    3. Repeat the procedure, but, as the child becomes more familiar with the activity, always give her a chance to do more on her own.

III. **Ending:** When Outside Time is nearly over, announce, *"Outside time is almost over."* Then a minute or two later say, *"Outside time is over."* Ask each child to stop playing, saying, *"Time to go inside."*

IV. **Suggestions:** With a child who does not respond, begin by playing yourself. Be sure he is attending to your actions. Make enthusiastic sounds to convey your pleasure in play. When you have aroused the child's interest, help him to imitate you. Try to get each child interested in a particular object or game. Allow him to make the first move when possible, moving in only to ensure that he is playing appropriately. With each child use language that is controlled and meaningful to his developmental stage.

SNACK TIME

CSID Learning Experience/Snack Time

Developmental Therapy Objective C-3/to respond to verbal stimulus and single object with a recognizable approximation of the appropriate verbal response

Area: Communication *Stage:* I *Name:* Juice and Cookies	*Cross-Reference Objectives:* Behavior 0–5 Communication 0–2 Socialization 1–4, 7 Academics 1–5
Materials/Special Instructions Different kinds of juice and cookies	*Support Teacher* Bring the children to the table if they need physical intervention to get them there. Direct the children to say or approximate "*juice*" and "*cookie*" each time they want more.

LEAD TEACHER

I. **Introduction:** *"It's snack time. I have juice and cookies. Come sit in chair."* Move to the table first, allowing the children to follow. Shake the container of juice and the bag of cookies to attract the children's attention.

II. **Step-by-step:**
1. Take the container of juice and raise it in the air or bang it on the table while loudly saying, *"Juice!"*
2. While you excitedly show the juice, have the support teacher pass out cups to each child.
3. Urge each child to say, *"Juice,"* or approximate the /j/ sound depending on the child's language abilities.
4. After the child has said the word or at least attempted the sound, give him some juice.
5. Show the children the bag of cookies and repeat Steps 3 and 4 of the above sequence.

III. **Ending:** When the children begin to lose interest, announce that *"Snack time is almost over."* When everyone has had enough, say, *"Snack time is over."*

IV. **Suggestions:** See the discussion of Snack Time in Part Two for a detailed description of this activity.

BATHROOM TIME

CSID Learning Experience/Bathroom Time

Developmental Therapy Objective B-5/to actively assist in learning self-help skills

Area: Behavior *Stage:* I *Name:* Toileting	*Cross-Reference Objectives:* Behavior 7, 9, 11–12 Communication 2, 4 Socialization 4, 7–8 Academics 4–6, 13, 16
Materials/Special Instructions None	*Support Teacher* This is an activity most effectively conducted by the support teacher while the lead teacher carries on the next planned activity (a simple one) with the remaining children.

LEAD TEACHER

I. **Introduction:** Announce to each child, "*It's bathroom time!*" (or another familiar phrase). You will usually carry on another simple activity (such as playing in a sand box) with the remainder of the children while the support teacher helps each child with toileting.

II. **Step-by-step (for the support teacher):**
1. If a child is just beginning potty training, undress him and put him on the toilet.
2. For a child who is partially trained, undress him part of the way and then let him finish. With a child wearing long pants, pull pants half way down and take one leg out. Let him take the other leg out. As the child progresses, let him take both legs out. Higher level children would be expected to pull pants down without assistance and without removing pants.
3. After the child has used the bathroom, appropriate praise is given. Assist him in pulling up his pants if he needs help.

III. **Ending:** The child then returns to the group.

IV. **Suggestions:** If boys are not tall enough to urinate standing on the floor, provide a box for them to stand on. If they cannot stand, seat them on the toilet facing the rear.

SAND OR WATER TIME

CSID Learning Experience/Water Time

Developmental Therapy Objective B-1/to react to sensory stimulus by attending toward source of stimulus by body response or by looking

Area: Behavior
Stage: I
Name: Basic Water Routine

Cross-Reference Objectives:
Behavior	0, 2–6
Communication	2–5
Socialization	5, 8–9
Academics	1–6, 8–9

Materials/Special Instructions
A water table mounted on legs so that it is as high as the children's waists or a large shallow pan. Provide playthings such as boats, rubber ducks, cups, straws, etc.

Support Teacher
There will be plenty of activity for both you and the lead teacher here. Work with several children while the lead teacher works with others. Model her motions and verbalization. Keep all children involved as the lead teacher moves from one to another. Use as much physical contact as needed to keep a child attending.

LEAD TEACHER

I. **Introduction:** Announce the activity. To gain the children's attention, uncover the water table and make short, sharp splashes on the surface of the water. *"Splash! Let's play in water."*

II. **Step-by-step:**
1. Position the children around the table.
2. Take each child's hand and move it through the motions of hitting the water to make a splash. Use selected words such as *"Splash! Play in water!"* constantly during the activity. Use other controlled vocabulary when suited.
3. Place wet fingers to the child's face and mouth and run wet hands along his arms.

III. **Ending:** Prepare to end the activity by saying, *"Water time is almost over."* Close the water table lid, saying, *"Water is all gone."* Attempt to get a response from all the children individually: *"Sue, say water is all gone."* Urge the children to dry themselves off by doing so yourself and saying, *"Let's dry hands."* Help those children who need it.

IV. **Suggestions:** Give the more advanced children floating toys. Let the children explore if they continue to be interested in the water.

CSID Learning Experience/Sand Time

Developmental Therapy Objective B-4/to respond with motor and body responses to complex environmental and verbal stimuli

Area: Behavior
Stage: I
Name: Basic Sand Routine

Cross-Reference Objectives:

Behavior	0–3, 6
Communication	2–5
Socialization	5, 8–9
Academics	1–6

Materials/Special Instructions
A sand box mounted on legs so that it is as high as the children's waists, sand, and toys such as trucks, cups, sifters, buckets, spoons, etc.

Support Teacher
Reflect what each child is doing or making in the sand. Redirect children who are using sand inappropriately (throwing it, eating it). Demonstrate actions (truck moving in sand) while describing them in simple language. Then give the children the toys so they can model you. If they cannot, motor them through the activity.

LEAD TEACHER

I. **Introduction:** Uncover the sand table and fill a bucket with sand. Pour the sand out slowly so the children can see it. *"I'm playing with sand. Come to sand time."*

II. **Step-by-step:**
1. As the children come to the sand table, assign a task to each one. *"Reginald, play with trucks in sand."* Pick a toy that is the child's favorite.
2. If a child does not respond to the directions, motor him through a demonstration of how to play with the toy in the sand. You may do this by making designs in the sand and letting some of it run through the child's fingers.

3. Use controlled vocabulary to reflect the child's action. Encourage the child to use these same words.

III. **Ending:** Say, *"Time to cover up sand!"* Help the children to hold the cover and place it on top of the sand table. Then encourage them to dust the sand from their hands by doing so yourself, saying, *"Let's clean hands."*

IV. **Suggestions:** If a child is afraid of the sand, take his hand and pour sand slowly over it. Smile and repeat, *"Sand feels good."* Lower level children may be unable to play in the sand with toys or make designs or objects such as cakes and pies. Have them do something very basic such as pouring sand from one container to another.

ART TIME

CSID Learning Experience/Art Time

Developmental Therapy Objective B-2/to respond to stimulus by sustained attending toward source of stimulus

Area: Behavior
Stage: I
Name: Shaving Cream

Cross-Reference Objectives:
Behavior   1, 3–5
Communication   1–3, 5
Socialization   1–4, 7–8
Academics   1, 3–6, 8

Materials/Special Instructions
Can of shaving cream (whipped topping can be used also), black construction paper (18″ × 24″ preferable), basin of warm water, paper towels

Support Teacher
Follow the model of the lead teacher with individual children. Help build interest with a soothing, soft voice and actions. Direct the children back to the lead teacher when she gives any cues or instructions.

LEAD TEACHER

I. **Introduction:** Hold up the black paper, rattling it, and say, *"Paper! Who wants paper?"* Try to obtain eye contact on verbalization while handing out a sheet of black paper to each child.

II. **Step-by-step:**
1. Bring the can of shaving cream very conspicuously into everyone's view. *"What's this?"* When everyone is attending, say, *"Cream!"* squirting out some in your hand in an enticing manner. ("Ooohing and aaahing" over the feeling is helpful.)
2. Then quickly smear it on a piece of black paper, continuing to react vocally to the tactile experience. *"Cream feels good! I'm drawing!"* The child who responds to the demonstration and wants cream should immediately have some squirted on his hand. *"Mike wants cream! He's ready to draw!"*

3. Then call each child's name as you put the cream on his hand. Keep the cream out of the children's eyes.
4. Let each child explore the cream *before* smearing it on paper. If no exploring takes place, motor him into this. Take his other hand and rub it against the cream, coating both hands as you lead him into finger painting.

III. **Ending:** After the children have participated successfully to some degree, end the art activity by asking for each child's paper. Then have paper towels and a container of warm water brought to the table.

IV. **Suggestions:** Exploring the warm water can be as stimulating and productive for the children as the actual art time. Motivate the higher level children to help wipe up the table. Give the same verbal clean-up request to the lower functioning children, but motor them through the process. Praise all positive actions with a hug.

CSID Learning Experience/Art Time

Developmental Therapy Objective C-3/to respond to verbal stimulus and single object with a recognizable approximation of the appropriate verbal response

Area: Communication *Stage:* I *Name:* Hole Punch Art	*Cross-Reference Objectives:* Behavior 0–3 Communication 0–2 Socialization 1–4 Academics 2–5

Materials/Special Instructions Single hole punch for each child and strips of construction paper	*Support Teacher* Direct the children to the lead teacher. If a child is not able to manipulate the hole punch and paper, hold his hand and move him through the activity. You may need to hold the paper while a child punches a hole. Verbalize to the child, *"Mike, you are punching holes!"*

LEAD TEACHER

I. **Introduction:** Take a hole punch and paper from the cabinet verbalizing, *"I have hole punch and p-a-p-e-r."* Then take the hole punch, slowly push the paper in, and punch holes so each child can watch the process. Hold the paper up saying, *"I punched holes!"* Punch a lot of holes and let the punched out circles fall rapidly to the table in front of the children.

II. **Step-by-step:**
1. For nonverbal children give each child a hole punch and sheet of paper, again verbalizing, *"Hole punch and paper."* Draw out the initial consonant sounds and encourage the children to imitate them. Verbal children are required to ask for items.

2. Give each child a strip of paper and a hole punch and ask him to punch holes, or motor him through the activity. *"Mike is punching holes!"*

III. **Ending:** As each child shows some understanding of the process and achieves success, ask for the materials back, praising the children individually. *"Look at circles we punched!"* Attempt to get the children to say the word *circles* while they are cleaning up.

IV. **Suggestions:** Ask the children to punch out a design on their sheets of paper. Then have them make another design by punching holes in a folded piece of paper. They can also take a string or yarn with masking tape wrapped around the ends and thread it through the holes they have punched.

CSID Learning Experience/Art Time

Developmental Therapy Objective C-5/to produce recognizable single words in several activities to obtain a desired response from an adult

Area: Communication *Stage:* I *Name:* Fingerpaint and Sand	*Cross-Reference Objectives:* Behavior 1–5, 7 Communication 1–2, 4, 7 Socialization 1–4, 8, 10 Academics 1–6, 9, 12

Materials/Special Instructions
Clear plastic container filled half-full of yellow fingerpaint (mix about 1/2 cup sand with paint to make a rough texture), paint smocks (one for each child and both teachers) or old shirts in correct sizes and buttoned on backward, fingerpaint paper (12" × 18")

Support Teacher
This is an activity that requires exceptional agility on the part of both you and the lead teacher. Follow through with the lead teacher's verbalizations in working with individual children. The idea is to have each child respond to the materials, even if only minimally. Try to help the children stay on the paper, to make some kind of movement with their hands, and to keep from putting paint into their mouths. Make interesting noises as they paint.

LEAD TEACHER

I. **Introduction:** *"We are painting today!"* Shake the paint container so sight and sound attract the children. Direct them to the table and assist them, if necessary, in sitting in their chairs. Pull bright colored smocks (shirts) out of the cabinet and say, *"We wear smocks (shirts) when we paint. What will we do?"* Provide a model for the answer if the child cannot respond with *paint*. Reinforce all verbal efforts with praise. Physically assist those children who cannot put on their smocks alone.

II. **Step-by-step:**
1. As the smocks are being put on, look for a child who is ready and hold up the paper in front of him. Say, *"Paper, pa—paper"* to elicit an appropriate response. (Use phrase, *"I want paper,"* for higher objective.) If only eye contact is expected, give paper and continue with next child.
2. Then hold up a clear container of yellow fingerpaint to which sand has been added to vary the texture from the usual smooth fingerpaint. Say, *"Paint, who wants paint?"* Elicit an appropriate response from each child. Give each child the opportunity to reach into the container and get a handful of paint. If he is reluctant to do this, put your hand in, get some out, and smear it on his paper. Make a line or some simple design and say, *"Look, Mike, paint!"*
3. Allow time for the child to put his hands into the paint by himself. If he makes no response, physically move his fingers or hand around in the paint. Work with individual children, along with the support teacher, and attempt to get at least *some* type of involvement from each.

III. **Ending:** After the children are involved in painting for a few minutes successfully, say, *"Art time is almost over."* Don't prolong the activity until they lose interest. Move to each child and help him make some movement in the paint. Then, say, *"Art time is over. Time to clean up."*

The support teacher gathers up all papers as you direct the children to the bathroom to wash the paint off their hands. Say, *"Wash hands."* Motor any children who need help through washing and drying their hands. After a child's hands have been washed, say, *"Take off smock."* If necessary, assist the child in taking off his smock.

IV. **Suggestions:**
1. Fingerpaint can be used without loss of motivation by varying the texture of the paint. Dry tempera powder can be sprinkled onto liquid starch or buttermilk. Other additives that change the texture are: Karo syrup—sticky; vegetable glue—gooey; lumpy flour and water—lumpy. You also can fingerpaint with instant pudding—different flavors. Children will want to taste it. Let them since you are attempting to stimulate as many sensory systems as possible in each activity.
2. If a child is reluctant to put his hand into the paint jar, try letting him get the paint out with a spoon.
3. Many schizophrenic children resist finger painting. They do not want to mess up their hands or clothes. Demonstrate, assuring them that it will wash off. It may be necessary for some children to paint with sticks or a spoon initially until they become more comfortable with the medium.
4. Use attractive neat containers rather than dirty containers with dry, caked paint on the edges and outside.
5. Encourage the children to paint in different ways—fingers, palm, wrist, arm, elbows, etc.
6. Encourage the children to move as much as possible. Demonstrate various ways to move your fingers to create simple but interesting designs. This is a good time to practice imitating circular and vertical strokes.

CSID Learning Experience/Art Time

Developmental Therapy Objective C-7/to produce a meaningful, recognizable sequence of words (without a model) to obtain a desired response from adults or children, or to label

Area: Communication *Stage:* I *Name:* Cream of Wheat Art	*Cross-Reference Objectives:* Behavior 1–4, 11–12 Communication 1–6 Socialization 1–4, 7–10 Academics 1–4, 6, 8–9

Materials/Special Instructions

Cream of wheat, water, container for water, large sheets of colored construction paper for each child. You will have to control water and cream of wheat. Be aware that some children will want to taste or eat the cream of wheat. Allow them to do so but then direct them back to the process wanted

Support Teacher

Direct the child to the lead teacher. Encourage each child to blow. Praise the child for responding. If the child puts cream of wheat in his mouth, redirect by saying, *"We are blowing."* Blow gently in the child's face, if necessary, to give him the idea.

LEAD TEACHER

I. **Introduction:** Announce the activity by saying, *"I have paper,"* dramatically waving paper for the children to see. Then take a container of water and sprinkle some water on the paper, verbalizing the process as you sprinkle. Then take some cream of wheat and pour a small pile on a dry part of the paper, saying, *"Blow!"* Gently blow the cream of wheat toward the water. Hold up the paper saying, *"See the picture?"* Give them all a chance to see it.

II. **Step-by-step:**
1. Ask children, *"What do you need?"* Then ask, *"What do you need next?"*
2. Paper is given first to children who respond by gesture, word, or sound. After each child has asked for paper and water and received them, pour a small pile of cream of wheat on each child's paper and encourage him to blow the cream of wheat on his paper. Provide verbal response models as needed.

3. If a child is reluctant to blow, go over to him saying, *"Blow."* Kneel down next to him and blow on his paper, exclaiming, *"Look! Now Joey blow!"*
4. A child may prefer to put his hands in the cream of wheat and spread it on the paper. Allow this, saying, *"Joey is using his hands."* However, continue to encourage him to blow. Sprinkle more water and then verbalize, *"Now let's blow."* Encourage the children to ask for more water and cream of wheat, saying, *"What do you want?"* and holding up needed material to help each child identify his needs.

III. **Ending:** At the appropriate time announce that the activity is almost over. Ask each child, *"What did you do?"* Provide response model when needed. Ask each child for his paper and give the child a damp paper towel for clean-up.

IV. **Suggestions:** Powdered Jell-o or Kool-Aid could also be used with the water.

CSID Learning Experience/Art Time

Developmental Therapy Objective A-15/to recognize several body parts (eye, hand, foot, nose, leg, arm, knee)

Area: Academics *Stage:* I *Name:* Masks	*Cross-Reference Objectives:* Behavior 4, 7, 9 Communication 1–4, 9 Socialization 1–4, 7 Academics 6–8, 11

Materials/Special Instructions

Paper plates, construction paper, markers. Have colored paper precut into the shapes of eyes, nose, mouths, etc. for the children. Use 2-oz. preopened glue bottles.

Support Teacher

Prepare materials and assist the children to the art area. Then, direct them to watch the lead teacher. Use the lead teacher's verbalizations, helping individual children during the activity. Be sure to give each enough opportunity to see how much he can do alone. Praise and nurture each child. Cue the lead teacher to admire individual successes. Remove materials as the lead teacher collects the masks.

LEAD TEACHER

I. **Introduction:** Holding a happy face in front of your chest (not over your face as it might frighten the children), announce, *"It's art time!"* Take the art supplies from the cabinet. *"I have paper plates. We are going to make masks!"* Demonstrate by putting the eyes and mouth on a plate and then pasting them on. Use yarn for the hair. As you put on each part, say, *"I'm putting on eyes (pause) and mouth to make a happy face."* You may touch your own and the children's bodies while verbalizing each body part. Ask the children, *"What is this?"* each time you put on a part. Provide a response model when needed.

II. **Step-by-step:**
1. Children with verbal skills can be required to say, *"I want plate."*
2. Children who are able to cut with scissors are given a sheet of construction paper with eyes and mouth drawn. Instruct them to cut them out.
3. For children not yet ready to learn to cut, these parts are already cut out. Move children who are unable to attend through the activity by saying, *"Put on eyes, put on mouth"* and then help them complete the task. Move each child's hand to the glue and then to the paper plate, saying to him, *"Use glue"* or *"You put on eyes! Good, Mike!"*
4. Encourage verbalization by asking the child, *"What is this?"* Point to eyes or mouth. Continue eliciting responses.

III. **Ending:** As each child finishes his mask, take him to the mirror. Assist him in holding up the mask to his face. Then, carefully take the mask away. Say, *"Mike, I see you!"*

IV. **Suggestions:** Nose, eyebrows, hair (yarn) can be used at later lessons when higher manipulative and conceptual skills are apparent.

CSID Learning Experience/Art Time

Developmental Therapy Objective A-17/to recognize several colors

Area: Academics *Stage:* I *Name:* Decorate the Tree	*Cross-Reference Objectives:* Behavior 0–4, 10 Communication 1–5 Socialization 1–4, 8 Academics 1–12
Materials/Special Instructions Large white sheet of butcher paper with the outline of a tree (one-foot high) drawn for each child and crayons	*Support Teacher* Assist in motoring the children through coloring. Encourage each child to make balls or other decorations on the tree. Praise the children for appropriate response.

LEAD TEACHER

I. **Introduction:** Cover the table with a large piece of paper on which a tree shape has been drawn for each child. Say, *"I have paper,"* placing the paper on the table. Again say, *"Paper!"* Then point to the tree, saying to each child, *"Tree. Let's color trees!"*

II. **Step-by-step:**
1. Hold two crayons (green and yellow) within the child's visual range and ask each child to pick a color.
2. Any reaching gesture or verbal attempt is rewarded with the crayon chosen. If there is no response, give the green crayon, saying, *"Color tree green."*
3. Assist children at a lower developmental level by helping them move crayons back and forth over their own tree saying, *"Look! Joey colored tree yellow."* Staying inside the line is not necessary.

III. **Ending:** Respond to each child's work emphasizing the color. Then assist the children in displaying their work on the wall. Children beginning to work on A-21, counting with one-to-one correspondence, can also count the trees.

IV. **Suggestions:** Advanced children can be given the opportunity to choose additional colors to use. Advanced children can be asked, *"What color do you have?"* or *"What color do you want?"*
This type of lesson can be done using flower shapes, Easter eggs, or simple shapes such as circles, squares, etc. Shapes will help develop line awareness and give concrete boundaries to children who can practice controlled coloring for eye-hand coordination.

MUSIC TIME

MUSIC TIME

CSID Learning Experience/Music Time

Developmental Therapy Objective B-3/to respond spontaneously to simple environmental stimulus with a motor behavior

Area: Behavior *Stage:* I *Name:* Rhythm Fun	*Cross-Reference Objectives:* Behavior 0–4 Communication 0–2, 4–5, 7 Socialization 1–4, 7–8, 10 Academics 1–6, 9, 12

Materials/Special Instructions Box decorated in bright red paper (large enough to hold six to eight rhythm instruments) and enough maracas so that each child and the lead teacher can have one. Variations of this exercise can serve as guides for music activities with almost any rhythm instrument.	*Support Teacher* Direct the children to the lead teacher. Encourage them to ask for maracas in a way appropriate for their level. Assist them in playing if necessary, saying, *"Shake! Shake!"*

LEAD TEACHER

I. **Introduction:** Direct the children to sit on the floor in the music area facing you. Take a maraca out of the box and shake it in front of the children. Say, *"Maraca. I have maracas."*

II. **Step-by-step:**

1. Hold a maraca in front of a child and say, *"Reginald, want maraca?"*

2. When the child reaches for the instrument, nods his head, or verbally responds to the question, give him the maraca. If a child does not respond when he is asked, place the instrument in his hands and gently assist him in playing it. Repeat Steps 1 and 2 until each child has a maraca.

3. Then sing a made-up song and play your maraca. *"I play my maraca and go shake, shake, shake...."* All the children should begin to play their maracas as you sing and play yours. You might add verses using each child's name, *"Reginald plays his maraca...,"* etc.

III. **Ending:** After the song is over, hold out the box and say, *"Put maracas in box."*

IV. **Suggestions:** This activity can be used to work on communication objectives at a higher level if the therapist says, *"I have maracas. Who wants maracas?"* The verbalization required for individual children should be determined by each child's objectives in communication. Some children may be expected to give eye contact; some may give a motor response (reaching); and some may be expected to say a sentence (*"I want maraca"*), a word (*"maraca"*) or an approximation (*m* sound). Hopefully, the activity will be so interesting that you can work up to having each child give some sort of response over a period of time.

CSID Learning Experience/Music Time

Developmental Therapy Objective B-4/to respond with motor and body responses to complex environmental and verbal stimuli

Area: Behavior
Stage: I
Name: Play the Cymbals

Cross-Reference Objectives:
Behavior   0–4
Communication   0–5, 7, 9
Socialization   1–4, 7–8, 10
Academics   1–6, 8

Materials/Special Instructions
Small cymbals for each child (or bells, sticks, flutes, kazoos, or other)

Support Teacher
Direct the children to the lead teacher encouraging them to ask for cymbals. Once each child has a pair of cymbals assist them in playing, encouraging them to imitiate lead teacher. If a child does not respond, motor him through the actions.

LEAD TEACHER

I. **Introduction:** Take the cymbals from a box filled with musical instruments. Say, *"I have cymbals,"* as you clang them together.

II. **Step-by-step:**
1. Ask, *"What do you want?"* Children with verbal skills are required to say, *"I want cymbals."* Each child is required to make the sound of which he is capable to receive cymbals.
2. If the child cannot respond verbally, encourage him to reach for the cymbals.
3. After each child has the cymbals, turn on a record and play along with the record or sing a simple song for them to accompany.
4. For a child who will not respond to clanging the cymbals, move the child's hands to make a sound with the cymbals.

III. **Ending:** After playing the cymbals, say, *"Put cymbals in box,"* as you extend the box to each child.

IV. **Suggestions:** Vary the activity by the use of different instruments, such as bells, sticks, flutes, kazoos, drums, and other instruments.

CSID Learning Experience/Music Time

Developmental Therapy Objective B-4/to respond with motor and body responses to complex environmental and verbal stimuli

Area: Behavior
Stage: I
Name: Play the Guitar

Cross-Reference Objectives:
Behavior   1–4, 7, 9, 11
Communication   1–5, 7
Socialization   1–4, 6–8, 10
Academics   1–6, 8–9

Materials/Special Instructions
One guitar (or autoharp), enough shakers for all the children, a pick, and a box covered with brightly colored paper to put the shakers in. The song in Step 6 is an adaptation of "Play Your Instruments and Make a Pretty Sound" from the record, *Play Your Instruments and Make a Pretty Sound,* by Ella Jenkins with Franz Jackson and his original Jazz All-Stars, distributed by Folkways Scholastic Records, copyright 1968 by Folkways Records and Service Corporation.

Support Teacher
Physically help the children with the shakers as needed. Play a shaker yourself and show pleasure in the activity. Redirect children as needed (see #3 under Suggestions).

LEAD TEACHER

I. **Introduction:** Direct the children to sit in a semicircle facing you in the music area. Put the guitar case in front of you and say, *"I have box."*

II. **Step-by-step:**
1. *"Let's open box."* Allow the children to help open the guitar case, but don't require it.
2. Take out the guitar and say, *"I have guitar."* Move the case away from the group.
3. Put the other box in front of you on the floor. Take a shaker out and say, *"Shaker!"*
4. Hold a shaker out to a child and say, *"This is shaker. What do you want?"* Give him the shaker when he approximates the word. Repeat with all but the last child. Move the box away from the group.
5. Hold out the guitar to the last child and say, *"Guitar. What do you want?"* When he approximates the word say, *"Play guitar!"*
6. Play the chords and sing the words below while the child strums. (Help children at first as they learn to strum.)
   Mike plays guitar and he makes a pretty sound.
   Mike plays guitar and he makes a pretty sound.
   Mike plays guitar and he makes a pretty sound.
   Mike makes a pretty sound.
7. Say, *"Mike, plays guitar!"*
8. Say to a child that has a shaker, *"Maria, give shaker to Mike. Good giving shaker, Maria. Come play guitar."*
9. Repeat Steps 5–9 until each child has played the guitar.

III. **Ending:**
1. Hold the box out to each child and say, *"Put shaker in box."* Praise each child for putting away his shaker by saying, *"Mike, puts shaker in box."* Move the box of shakers away from the group.
2. Put the guitar case on the floor in front of you. Put the guitar in the case, saying, *"Put guitar in box."* Allow children to help close the case as you say, *"Let's close box."* Move the guitar away from the group.

IV. **Suggestions:**
1. As the lead teacher, your right hand is free even though you are holding the guitar. Use this hand to help a child strum if needed. Also use it to touch the other children who are playing the shakers so that they don't feel you've abandoned them.
2. The guitar is a very motivating instrument, and all the children may want to be touching the guitar rather than playing the shakers. Unless the children are working or waiting and taking turns, you may want to allow this. At Stage One it's often a sign of progress when they show such an interest. Children beginning to move into Stage Two, however, may be working on Behavior-9. In this case it is primarily the support teacher's responsibility to redirect a child back to his shaker.
3. Some children are more motivated by a shaker in each hand. This provides a more nearly total body response.
4. You can also do this activity with an autoharp or drum. When using a large drum, two children can play the drum at the same time.

CSID Learning Experience/Music Time

Developmental Therapy Objective B-4/to respond with motor and body responses to complex environmental and verbal stimuli

Area: Behavior	*Cross-Reference Objectives:*
Stage: I	Behavior 0–3, 7
Name: Play the Tambourine	Communication 1–5, 7
	Socialization 1–4, 8, 10
	Academics 1–4, 6, 8–9

Materials/Special Instructions

Tape player, tambourines, large box covered with brightly colored paper, "Classical Gas" by Mason Williams, Warner Brothers Records. This activity may be varied for other types of instruments or music activities.

Support Teacher

Direct the children toward the lead teacher. Help the child individually, as needed, to model the lead teacher. Praise the children for responding, always showing pleasure with the entire music activity.

LEAD TEACHER

I. **Introduction:** Direct the children to the music area and seat them facing you. Take a tambourine out of the box and shake it in front of the children. Say, *"Tambourine!"*

II. **Step-by-step:**

1. Hold a tambourine in front of each child, saying, *"What is this?"* As each child gives the expected response, reaches for it, nods his head, or verbally responds to the question, give him a tambourine. Repeat until each child has a tambourine.

2. Turn on the tape player. Hold the tambourine in front of you with both hands, shake it, and say, *"Do this!"* All the children should begin to shake their tambourines, modeling the teacher. If any child is unable to imitate immediately, put your hand over his and help him shake the tambourine. Pull away occasionally to see if the child can follow the motions on his own.

3. After about 12 beats say, *"Stop!"* It may be necessary to physically help some children stop by placing your hand on their tambourine or on their hand and saying, *"Stop."* Smile and say, *"You stopped."* Stop playing your tambourine and get eye contact with the children. When they are all looking and have stopped playing, change the location of the tambourine. Shake it above your head (still holding it with two hands) and say, *"Do this!"* Hopefully, all the children will begin to shake their tambourines above their heads, modeling the teacher. Follow the same procedure above with children who cannot imitate immediately.

4. Repeat Step 3 four times, varying the location of the tambourine: hold the tambourine with two hands, shake it on your lap, hit it on your legs. Then, shake it above your head and in front of your body again.

III. **Ending:** Say, *"Stop!"* Turn off the tape recorder. Hold out the box and say, *"Put tambourines in box."*

IV. **Suggestions:**

1. Holding the tambourine with both hands gives the child more control and helps him focus on the shaking. The activity is too easy to tune out when shaking the tambourine with one hand (only the hand and arm movements are involved), but when the child uses both hands, the shaking movement involves a more nearly total body response (arms, head, and upper torso).

2. Initially keep the number of changes in the location of tambourine shaking to a minimum to limit the number of complex motor responses you are demanding. Too many different ones at first will confuse the child.

3. Do not change the location movements too quickly. Twelve beats are usually sufficient, but be sure all children are participating and have made the physical change to that location before you say *"Stop"* and move to a new location for them to model.

4. In the initial passing out of the instruments, it may be necessary to touch a child to get his attention if he does not respond when you call his name. Place the tambourine in his hands and gently assist him in playing it.

CSID Learning Experience/Music Time

Developmental Therapy Objective B-9/to wait without physical intervention by adult

Area: Behavior **Stage:** II **Name:** "Are You Sleeping?"	***Cross-Reference Objectives:*** Behavior 8, 11–12 Communication 9–11, 13 Socialization 13–15, 18 Academics 18, 31
Materials/Special Instructions Small rug or pallet, sheet or blanket, small hand bell, ukelele. The song is a modification of "Are You Sleeping?"	***Support Teacher*** Model the activity for the child. Be enthusiastic as you model to increase motivation and level of awareness. Assist each child as he takes a turn, if necessary, and keep others directed toward the lead teacher.

LEAD TEACHER

I. **Introduction:** *"Now it's music time."* The support teacher has put out a rug, sheet, ukelele, and bell. The support teacher comes over with the group and goes to bed (she lies down on the rug). Say, *"Sh! Ms. _____ is going to sleep,"* and pull the sheet up over the support teacher to cover her. Pat the support teacher on the back and say, *"Goodnight Ms. _____;"* give her a hug. Move back to the group (like someone tiptoeing away from a sleeping baby) while the support teacher pretends to be asleep. *"Sh! Ms. _____ is asleep."*

II. **Step-by-step:**
1. Pick up the ukelele and sing in a quiet voice, *"Are you sleeping, are you sleeping, Ms. _____?"* Stop, turn to group and quietly say, *"It's time for her to wake up. Let's clap."*
2. Start clapping hands (like slow bells ringing—two beats to a measure) as you sing *"Morning bells are ringing, morning bells are ringing. Ding, ding, dong. Ding, ding, dong."*
3. As you start clapping and singing with the children, the support teacher (who has been cued ahead of time) looks surprised, sits up in bed, picks up the bell, and starts ringing it. Say, *"Ms. _____ woke up!"*
4. The support teacher moves to a child and says, *"Reginald, it's time to go to bed."* She leads that child to the rug and he lies down. Repeat the activity as described in the above introduction—Step 2 for the support teacher. Substitute the child's name in all appropriate places including, *"Are you sleeping, are you sleeping, Brother Reginald,"* etc.
5. *"Now it's Reginald's turn to go to sleep,"* or *"Reginald, do you want to sleep?"*

6. As that child is moving to the bed, praise the remaining children for waiting in turn. This verbal support will set a positive tone and facilitate anxious children in being able to sit and wait. It also serves as a reminder to each of them that they will have a turn and that you haven't forgotten them. After a child has had a turn, you can praise him for waiting and watching *"Reginald have a turn."*
7. Repeat until each child has had a turn role playing the song.

III. **Ending:** *"Now that everybody's up out of bed . . . Listen . . . (pick up bell and ring it). I hear a bell ringing. It says everyone is awake."*

IV. **Suggestions:**
1. Be sure to involve all the children in the suspense of being very quiet while the child is sleeping and clapping when he wakes up; this will minimize the amount of physical intervention you must use and help them exercise their ability to wait for a turn.
2. This activity gives the lead teacher a chance to provide a special kind of nurturing to each child. She pulls the sheet up over him and gives him a hug as she tells him good night. This is a very caring gesture—to tuck a child into bed. Children who may not seek contact with an adult spontaneously—socialization milestone for Stage One—may be able to accept nurturing in a role play situation like this.
3. If a child has trouble picking another child, ask, *"Who hasn't had a turn yet?"* Then say, *"Reginald, Mike hasn't had a turn. You can tell him it's time to go to bed."*

CSID Learning Experience/Music Time

Developmental Therapy Objective C-3/to respond to verbal stimulus and single object with a recognizable approximation of the appropriate verbal response

Area: Communication
Stage: I
Name: Making Music

Cross-Reference Objectives:
Behavior   0–4
Communication   0–2, 4–5, 7
Socialization   1–4, 7–8, 10
Academics   1–6, 8–9

Materials/Special Instructions
Autoharp and pick
Song: Listen to _____ play the
       harp, play the harp,
       play the harp.
       Listen to _____ play the
       harp, play the harp.
(To the tune of "Here We Go 'Round the Mulberry Bush")

Support Teacher
Help individual children attend to the activity. Use the lead teacher's verbalizations, repeating to individual children. Help them get interested in the instrument by looking at and exploring it. Try to communicate excitement in actions and words. Use praise when each responds.

LEAD TEACHER

I. Introduction: Bring out the autoharp case and say, *"Look!"* Take out the autoharp and say, *"This is a harp."* Strum it enthusiastically.

II. Step-by-step:
1. Ask, *"What is this?"* If there is no response, say, *"Harp! This is a harp. Mike, say harp."*
2. After the child has looked at you and attempted to say the word, give him an autoharp pick and help him strum as you sing a song. The support teacher should direct the other children toward the autoharp, possibly helping them to clap.
3. After a verse is completed, reflect, *"Mike played the harp."* You may also say, *"Mike, give me pick,"* if the word pick has been introduced.
4. Repeat with the other children.

III. Ending: After all the children have had a turn, say, *"Bye-bye harp,"* as you put it in the case, or, *"Put harp in box."* You may also direct the children to help by saying, *"Mike, put in box."*

IV. Suggestions: Give each child a chance to play the instrument. Keep the autoharp near all of the children so they can also be aroused by watching or touching it while someone else is playing. The vibration caused by the strings may aid in motivation. Remember that waiting for a turn is a much higher level objective.

CSID Learning Experience/Music Time

Developmental Therapy Objective C-3/to respond to verbal stimulus and single object with a recognizable approximation of the appropriate verbal response

Area: Communication
Stage: I
Name: Mm, Mm, Good

Cross-Reference Objectives:
Behavior   0–7, 9, 11–12
Communication   0–3, 5
Socialization   1–3, 7–8, 12, 14
Academics   1–6, 8, 10, 12

Materials/Special Instructions
Four pictures of foods familiar to the children and a box to put the pictures in. The song in Step 4 is an adaptation of the Campbell Soup Song.

Support Teacher
Sing with the lead teacher. Help individual children stay involved in the activity. If they become distracted or just "tuned out," direct them toward the pictures, saying, *"Look! Pictures!"* When the lead teacher holds up different pictures, react with excitement. Rub your tummy when singing, *"Mm, mm, good;"* lick your lips, etc.

LEAD TEACHER

I. **Introduction:** Direct the children to sit in a semicircle in the music area. Display the box and say, *"I have pictures."*

II. **Step-by-step:**
 1. Hold up the first picture and say, *"What is this?"*
 2. Praise verbally and with touch those children who give the correct answer.
 3. Get eye contact with those who do not respond. Hold the picture just below your mouth. Say, *"This is apple. What is this?"* Give praise for approximation.

 4. Sing, *"Mm, mm, good; Mm, mm, good. That's what apple is. Mm, mm, good."*
 5. Praise those children who have tried to sing with you.
 6. Repeat sequence with another child.

III. **Ending:** Put pictures in box, saying, *"All are mm, mm, good!"*

IV. **Suggestions:** With higher level children, vary by letting each child draw a picture from the surprise box and tell the group what is *"Mm, mm, good."*

CSID Learning Experience/Music Time

Developmental Therapy Objective S-18/to participate in cooperative activities or projects with another child during organized class activities

Area: Socialization
Stage: II
Name: Having Fun in Music

Cross-Reference Objectives:
Behavior   11–12
Communication   11–13
Socialization   15
Academics   6, 10, 13

Materials/Special Instructions
This is an example of an activity that serves as a closing exercise for music time. The song is to the tune of "Mary Had a Little Lamb."
Song: We had fun in music, music, music.
        We had fun in music, music today!

Support Teacher
Be part of pair if needed, depending on the number of children. If you are not a partner, stay close to a pair and praise them verbally and with touch. Sing along with the lead teacher.

LEAD TEACHER

I. **Introduction:** Begin to sing, *"We had fun in music."* Turning to each child quickly, hold his hands and swing his arms in rhythm. Put the children in pairs. Each pair stands face-to-face. Say, *"Hold hands."* As always, move in to help children who need assistance.

II. **Step-by-step:**
   1. As verse is repeated, turn each child to the nearest partner, assisting the children, when needed, to hold hands and swing in rhythm while they sing. Select one child for your partner.

   2. All change partners and repeat Step 1. Repeat until you have been each child's partner.
   3. Direct the children to sit in a circle and say, *"Hold hands."* Sing, *"We had fun in music,"* as all swing arms.

III. **Ending:** Say, *"Music time is over."*

IV. **Suggestions:** Depending on the children's abilities, you might start with the verse given above and then add variations at later music periods as the children begin to respond.

CSID Learning Experience/Music Time

Developmental Therapy Objective A-11/to match similar objects with different attributes

Area: Academics
Stage: II
Name: Play the Sticks

Cross-Reference Objectives:
Behavior   0–4
Communication   1–5, 7
Socialization   1–5, 7–8, 10
Academics   1–4, 6, 9, 12

Materials/Special Instructions
Musical instruments: tambourines, sticks, or cow bells. Use one type of instrument for the group at a time. Have the other instruments in a box out of the children's sight. Children sit in a semicircle on the floor facing the lead teacher.

Support Teacher
Direct the children to the lead teacher, encouraging them to ask for the sticks. If a child does not hit the sticks, move him through and then gently pull away to see if he will continue hitting them. If he does not continue, move him through the process again.

LEAD TEACHER

I. **Introduction:** Hold up the sticks and hit them excitedly, saying, *"Watch and listen. These sticks make music!"*

II. **Step-by-step:**
1. Try to entice the child to ask for the sticks. Ask, *"Who wants the sticks?"* Children with verbal skills are required to say, *"I want sticks,"* or an approximation.
2. Nonverbal children may reach for the sticks or show other indications of wanting them.
3. Begin hitting the sticks and singing a simple song such as "This is the Way We Play the Sticks" to the tune of "Here We Go 'Round the Mulberry Bush,"

indicating for the children to join in. If they do not respond, gently motor them through the desired response. Move the sticks to the side, on the floor, and directly in front of each child, moving them constantly to keep each child involved.

III. **Ending:** After playing the sticks, ask each child for his, saying, *"Joey, give me the sticks."*

IV. **Suggestions:** Have each child hit another child's sticks. You might lay five sticks on the floor, saying, *"Let's count the sticks. John, count the sticks—1, 2, 3, 4, 5."* Point to each and help where needed. Continue with other children, varying the number of sticks.

CSID Learning Experience/Music Time

Developmental Therapy Objective A-15/to recognize several body parts

Area: Academics *Stage:* I *Name:* "Clap Your Hands"	*Cross-Reference Objectives:* Behavior 1–4, 7, 11 Communication 0–3 Socialization 1–4, 7 Academics 1–4, 6–7, 10
Materials/Special Instructions Arrange small carpet mats on the music area floor in a semicircle. The song is an adaptation of "Clap Your Hands" from the record, *American Folk Songs for Children,* copyright 1954 by Folkways Records and Service Corporation.	*Support Teacher* Move the children through the activity as needed. Direct the children's attention to the lead teacher. Praise individual children for their specific appropriate responses. If a child moves away from the activity area, try to lure him back with the music activities. If this does not work, lead him back and try to get him involved.

LEAD TEACHER

I. **Introduction:** Direct the children to sit on the mats. *"Let's clap hands!"*

II. **Step-by-step:**
1. Sing:
   Clap, clap, clap your hands,
   Clap your hands together
   Clap, clap, clap your hands,
   Clap your hands together.
   Repeat while singing, clap your hands, and help children clap as needed. Say, *"Good clapping hands!"*
2. Then say, *"Now, pat legs. Where are your legs, Maria?"* Praise each child who touches her legs by saying, *"Good, Maria. Legs!"*
3. Sing as you slap the top of your thighs. *"Pat, pat, pat your legs,"* etc. *"Good patting legs!"*
4. Repeat Steps 1–3 for *head, nose, mouth, eyes,* etc.

III. **Ending:** As a closing, sing:
Take, take, take your mat,
Take your mat together, etc.,
and direct children to pick up their mats and put them away while singing.

IV. **Suggestions:**
1. Some children need help locating their different body parts. You can physically move these children through the activity at first, and then give them a chance to try it by themselves again. Sometimes a mirror also helps, although this varies with each child.
2. Instead of saying, *"Where are your legs?,"* you might say, *"Show me your legs!"*
3. Since there are several verses, some children tune out. If this happens, you may want to reduce the number of verses and/or change the volume of your voice for each verse.

CSID Learning Experience/Music Time

Developmental Therapy Objective A-15/to recognize several body parts

Area: Academics *Stage:* I *Name:* "Put Your Hands Up in the Air"	*Cross-Reference Objectives:* Behavior 0–4, 11–12 Communication 0–4, 9 Socialization 1–3, 7 Academics 1–4, 6, 8, 10

Materials/Special Instructions Record player, the song, "Put Your Hands Up in the Air," *Learning Basic Skills Through Music,* Vol. 1, by Hap Palmer, Educational Activities, Inc., copyright 1969, Activity Records.	*Support Teacher* Participate in the activity. Direct the children's attention to the lead teacher. Provide help for individual children who need this. Move the child's hand when he is not able to respond. Remember to pull back occasionally to see how much the child will follow through on his own.

LEAD TEACHER

I. **Introduction:** Say, *"Let's stand up."*

II. **Step-by-step:**
1. Say, *"Listen to the music. Let's do what it says. Let's put hands up,"* as you model for the children.
2. Begin the record, following the directions. Verbalize what is sung on the record to help those who don't understand.

III. **Ending:** The last movement is "going back to your seat." This makes a good transition to the next activity on your schedule. If you want the children to stay in the music area, say, *"Sit on floor,"* or stop the record before this point.

IV. **Suggestions:** At one point in the song instructions are to "put your right hand up in the air." Unless the children are developmentally ready to learn right-left discrimination, it is best to say, *"One hand up."* For Stage One children it is best to sing the song yourself rather than use the record so you can slow it down to their pace.

GOOD-BYE TIME

CSID Learning Experience/Good-bye Time

Developmental Therapy Objective A-6/to imitate simple, familiar actions of adult upon request

Area: Academics *Stage:* I *Name:* Good-bye Song	*Cross-Reference Objectives:* Behavior 3–5, 7 Communication 1–2, 4, 7 Socialization 1–2, 6–7, 12, 15 Academics 3, 4, 6, 10, 12
Materials/Special Instructions A record or tape of "London Bridge" or any other familiar song	*Support Teacher* Direct the child to the lead teacher. She moves the children through the activity when necessary. You can use sight of a tape recorder or record player as a visual aid for children. Recorded music is not necessary but if it is used have record ready for the lead teacher by her chair.

LEAD TEACHER

I. **Introduction:** Announce the activity. Then say, *"Let's go sit in chairs."*

II. **Step-by-step:**
1. Sing, *"Now it's time to say good-bye, say good-bye, say good-bye. Now it's time to say good-bye, say good-bye."* Then ask the children to say *"good-bye"* to each other.
2. Sing another verse, substituting *wave* for *say*. Then ask the children to wave *good-bye* to each other. *"Mike, wave bye-bye to Joey!"* You might ask them to wave to you also.

III. **Ending:** As the song ends, get up, go to the door, and as a model for the children, put on a sweater or hat (weather permitting). Urge each child to do the same: *"Maria, time to go. Come get coat."* As the children leave the building, encourage them to say *"good-bye"* to the other school staff.

IV. **Suggestions:** To vary the activity, use different songs and substitute other actions such as *hug* and *shake* for *say* and *wave*.

appendix a

DEVELOPMENTAL THERAPY CURRICULUM OBJECTIVES

The Developmental Therapy objectives are 146 developmental milestones that promote emotional growth. They are sequenced for five stages of therapy and according to four curriculum areas: Behavior, Communication, Socialization, and (Pre)Academics.

Only the objectives for the first two stages are included in this appendix, because these stages encompass the developmental milestones necessary for the young autistic child.

For specific instructions in using the objectives as a criterion-referenced evaluation procedure, the reader is referred to Chapter Two of *Developmental Therapy,* Mary M. Wood, editor. For technical information concerning the validity of the objectives and other evaluation data, see Chapter Three in *Developmental Therapy.*

Behavior Objectives

STAGE I:
Responding to the Environment with Pleasure

STAGE I BEHAVIOR GOAL: TO TRUST OWN BODY AND SKILLS

■ 0. to indicate *awareness* of a sensory stimulus with *any responses* away from or toward source of stimulus (in situations with tactile, motor, visual, auditory, taste, or smell stimuli). Child must have two out of six modalities.
Examples:
Child responds when:
 a. *Teacher touches child's cheek (tactile).*
 b. *Teacher picks up child (motor).*
 c. *Teacher claps hands out of sight (auditory).*
 d. *Presented with strong odor (smell).*
 e. *Child puts objects in mouth (taste).*
 f. *Child follows moving object with eyes (visual).*

■ 1. to *react* to sensory stimulus by *attending* toward source of stimulus by body response or by looking (in situations using tactile, motor, visual, auditory, taste, or smell stimuli). (Same as academic objective A-1.) Child must have two out of six modalities.
Examples:
 a. *After teacher blows bubbles, child attends briefly by looking or responding with body language (visual stimulus).*
 b. *When teacher starts to play guitar, child attends briefly by turning head to source of sound, looking at guitar or teacher, or smiling (auditory stimulus).*
 c. *When teacher places child's hand in water, child indicates awareness by splashing or clapping hands together, withdrawing hands, or looking briefly at water (tactile stimulus).*

■ 2. to respond to stimulus by *sustained attending* toward source of stimulus (continued looking at object or person after initial stimulus-response has occurred). (Same as academic objective A-2.)
Examples:
 a. *After initial stimulus, child continues to watch teacher strum guitar during a song or continues to smile or move body to music.*
 b. *Child continues to look at or play in water.*

■ 3. to respond spontaneously to *simple* environmental *stimulus* with a motor behavior: object, person, sound. (Same as academic objective A-3.)
Examples:
 a. *Child sees block, picks it up, and throws it.*
 b. *Teacher holds out guitar. Child explores it.*
 c. *Teacher turns on music box (out of child's view). Child comes to see.*

■ 4. to respond with motor and body responses to *complex* environmental and verbal *stimuli* (through imitation "Do this;" through completion of verbal direction; or through minimal participation in activities) *given physical intervention and verbal cues.* (Same as academic objective A-4.)
Examples:
 a. *Parent says, "It's time to play in the water." Parent puts her hands in the water and splashes (to show child what to do). Then child puts hands in the water and splashes.*
 b. *Teacher says, "This is a boat. Let's push it." Teacher pushes boat as example. Child does not respond, so teacher places child's hand on boat. Then child begins to play with boat. Teacher says, "Good, you're playing with the boat" and pats child on the back.*
 c. *Teacher announces, "It's play time." Child gets up but is not sure in which direction to move. Teacher steers child (with hand on back) to play area. Child sits down in play area but doesn't initiate play, so teacher hands child a toy. Child takes toy.*

■ 5. to actively *assist* in learning *self-help skills* (toileting, washing hands, dressing, putting arms in coat when held). (Should be based upon chronological age expectations in combination with developmental expectations, mastery not essential.)
Examples:
 a. *Child indicates need to use bathroom (verbal or nonverbal); tries to pull down pants.*
 b. *Child tries to turn on water; puts hands under water; tries to use soap.*
 c. *Child pulls up pants or tries to button pants.*

■ 6. to respond *independently* to several play materials. (Verbal cues may be used; age-appropriate play is not necessary.) Perseverative or self-stimulatory behavior not acceptable.

Examples:

a. *Child spontaneously picks up a doll, holds it, rubs hair, moves doll's limbs (but does not rock baby, try to take doll's clothes off, or put baby in bed as would be expected of a child that age).*

b. *Child picks up block, puts it to his mouth, then throws it down.*

■ 7.   to indicate *recall* of class and home *routine* by moving *spontaneously* to next activity area without physical stimulus; verbal cues or touch may be used.

This objective is intended to help organize a child to the extent that when the activity is announced, the child is aware enough of the routine to move to the next activity.

Examples:

a. *When teacher says, "It's play time," child moves to play area without having to be physically moved by teacher.*

b. *Teacher says, "It's music time." Child gets up, starts in wrong direction. Teacher touches child and says again, "It's music time." Child moves to music area.*

c. *Teacher says, "It's time to go." Child goes to closet to get coat.*

STAGE II:
Responding to the Environment with Success

STAGE II BEHAVIOR GOAL: *TO SUCCESSFULLY PARTICIPATE IN ROUTINES AND ACTIVITIES*

■ 8. to use play materials *appropriately*, simulating normal play experience.
Child plays with toys with awareness of their function, both as representative, real-life objects (play stove for cooking), as well as objects for pretending (play stove turned over makes a castle wall). He does not see toys as objects to be destroyed but as objects that he uses to facilitate his fantasy or to play out real-life situations. If a child has difficulty discriminating reality from fantasy, it would not be appropriate for the child to continually pretend.
Examples:
   a. Child drives toy car up to service station and pretends to get gas.
   b. Child feeds and dresses a doll.
■ 9. to *wait* without physical intervention by adult. (Verbal support or touch may be used.) (Same as socialization objective S-14.)
Examples:
   a. Child races up to roll on the mats but is out of turn. Teacher says, "Wow, you are really happy about having mat time! I can't wait to see how well you do your cartwheel after Ricky finishes." Child goes in turn.
   b. Mike wants the cookies, and he wants them NOW. Teacher says, "You can have a cookie after John." Mike is able to wait.
   c. Child wants his turn first at kickball. Teacher says, "I remember that fly ball you caught yesterday. You were standing right here." Or, "Everyone gets a chance to kick and catch. It's your turn to catch now." Child moves to field.
   d. Child runs out of the room ahead of the group. Teacher says, "Wait at the door." Child waits.
■10. to *participate* in *sitting* activities such as Work Time, Story Time, Talking Time, Snack Time without physical intervention by adult. (Child is able to take part in the activities *by staying in the activity area, responding to materials,* and *following adult's directions* when given verbal support or touch by adult.) (Child's sitting per se is not the focus.)
Examples:
   a. Child moves away from story circle. Teacher exclaims and points to the book, "Wow, look at that huge wolf's teeth!" Child moves back into circle.
   b. Child moves in and out of chair during Work Time. Teacher says, "This work is easy when you're sitting in your chair." (Important then to support child during completion of work.) Child continues work to completion.
   c. Child begins to pour milk on the table. Teacher says, "Kids drink their milk here." Child stops pouring milk.
   d. Child runs away from the table. Teacher says, "We sit for art time." Child comes back to table. Or, teacher gets up, touches child on the back, then points to the table. Child comes back.
■11. to *participate* in *movement* activities such as Play Time, Mat Time, Games, Music, or Art Time without physical intervention by adult. (Child is able to take part in the activities *by staying in the activity area, responding to materials,* and *following adult's directions* when given verbal support or touch by adult.)
Examples:
   a. Child is reluctant to go through transition and, instead of going to Play Time, remains apart from group. Teacher says, "When you come to the play area, you'll get to play with the doll." Child moves to play area.
   b. Child loses control and threatens another child physically. Teacher moves between two children and says, "I know you want that truck, but I hear a big, red fire engine trying to get out of the toy cabinet." Child ceases fight and goes to toy cabinet.
   c. Child yells out words of a song very loudly, instead of singing, during music time. Teacher turns to other child who is singing appropriately and says, "Your soft voice sounds so pretty." Child stops yelling.
■12. to *spontaneously participate* in activities without physical intervention. (Verbal support or touch may be used, but child indicates some personal initiative to participate in every activity except transitions.)
Examples:
   a. Teacher says, "It's work time." Child picks up work folder (if that is the routine previously set up).
   b. During Snack Time and before Play Time, children begin discussing what they will play during Play Time, indicating that they know routine. Child subsequently moves to play.
   c. Teacher says that Play Time is almost over. Child begins to bring his play to closure and realizes that it is time to put toys away. Child begins putting toys away.

Communication Objectives

STAGE I:
Responding to the Environment with Pleasure

STAGE I COMMUNICATION GOAL: *TO USE WORDS TO GAIN NEEDS*

- 0. to *produce sounds* (child must master *c.* below to master objective).
  Examples:
    - a. *Child makes undifferentiated sounds.*
    - b. *Child vocalizes combinations of consonants and vowels.*
    - c. *Child repeats his own pattern of vocalizing for social or adaptive expression (several patterns desirable):*
        - *1) eee, nnnn, ahhh*
        - *2) ba ba, da da da, du gu du*
- 1. to *attend* to person speaking. (Child moves or looks toward adult when adult initiates verbal stimulus. Eye contact not necessary.)
  Example:
    > *Teacher greets children as they arrive. "Here is Johnny." Johnny directs his body or eyes toward teacher, or he may smile without looking directly at teacher.*
- 2. to *respond* to verbal stimulus with a *motor behavior* (Object present; teacher does not use gestures).
  Examples:
    - a. *Teacher says, "Ball." Child shows recognition by looking, touching, or body movement toward ball.*
    - b. *Teacher says, "Bye-bye." Child waves.*
- 3. to *respond* to verbal stimulus and single object with a *recognizable approximation of the appropriate verbal response.* (Child gives verbal approximation to indicate use or correct answer to question, "What is this?" Object present; function or name acceptable.)
  Examples:
    - a. *Teacher says, "Ball." Child attempts a "b" sound.*
    - b. *Teacher says, "What is this?" (milk). Child says, "Mi."*
      (Teacher may have to repeat the word for the child before the child makes the approximation.)
    - c. *Teacher says, "What do you want?" (scissors). Child says, "Cuh-cuh."*
- 4. to *voluntarily* use *recognizable single word approximations* in several activities to describe or label a situation, object, or event. (Child produces recognizable approximation spontaneously, e.g., "wa-wa" for water.) (Same as academic objective A-9.)
  Examples:
    - a. *Parent puts milk on the table, and child spontaneously says, "Mi, mi."*
    - b. *Teacher blows bubbles, saying, "I have bubbles, bubbles." As teacher begins blowing bubbles again, child excitedly attempts to say, "Bu, bu."*
    - c. *Child sees car going down street. Child says, "Ca."*
    - d. *Teacher is hopping, encouraging children to model. She is saying, "Hop-hop-hop-hop." Suddenly child says, "Op, op."*
- 5. to produce *recognizable single words* in several activities to obtain a *desired response from adult* or to label object for adult (e.g., "water" instead of "wa-wa" for water). (Verbal cues may be used.)
  Examples:
    - a. *Teacher puts milk on the table, and child says, "Milk."*
    - b. *At art time, teacher is holding art materials. Teacher says, "I have paper. Do you want paper?" Child says, "Paper! Paper!" Teacher gives child paper.*
    - c. *Child takes music box out of toy cabinet and holds it up to the teacher, saying, "Box."*
- 6. to produce *recognizable single words* in several activities to obtain a *desired response from another child* or to label for child. (Verbal cues may be used.)
  Examples:
    - a. *At play time, child sees another child with his favorite truck. He walks up and says, "Truck."*
    - b. *Child A tries to sit in child B's chair. B begins to get upset. Teacher says, "Tell him to move." B says, "Move."*
- 7. to produce a *meaningful*, recognizable *sequence of words* in several activities (without a model) to obtain a desired response from adults or children, or to label. (Gestures or verbal cues may be used.)
  Examples:
    - a. *Child says, "I want a cookie."*
    - b. *Child starts to take toy away from another child. Teacher says, "Ask him for it." Child says, "Give me that truck!"*
    - c. *Child says to teacher, "Go away."*
    - d. *Child sings a simple song.*
    - e. *Child says, "Me big fire truck."*

STAGE II:
Responding to the Environment with Success

STAGE II COMMUNICATION GOAL: *TO USE WORDS TO AFFECT OTHERS IN CONSTRUCTIVE WAYS*

■ 8. to *answer* a child's and an adult's *questions* or *requests* with *recognizable*, meaningful, relevant *word(s)*. (Response does not have to be accurate or constructive.)
Examples:
   a. *Child A says, "Give me that truck." Child B says, "This is my truck."*
   b. *Teacher says, "Would you like another cookie?" Child says, "I don't want your old cookie!"*
   c. *Teacher says, "What is this?" Child says, "Ball."*
■ 9. to exhibit a *receptive vocabulary* no more than two years behind chronological age expectations (as indicated by the PPVT or other means).
Example:
   The child comprehends what others are saying even if he does not talk (gesture or words acceptable).
■10. to *label simple feelings* in pictures, dramatic play, art, or music: *sad, happy, angry, afraid* (by gesture or word).
Examples:
   a. *Teacher shows picture of child crying and asks, "Is he sad or happy?" Child says, "Sad."*
   b. *Teacher shows two pictures and asks, "Which is sad?" Child points to correct choice.*
   c. *Child paints picture and says, "This is a mean picture."*
■11. to use simple word *sequences* to command or request of another child or adult in ways *acceptable to classroom procedures*. (Bizarre language content or socially inappropriate word sequences are not acceptable; behavior is not a consideration.)
Example:
   Child can say to teacher or another child, "I want your red color," or "Give me milk." If child uses loud or whiney voice, teacher can repeat more appropriately, and child will say it again modeling teacher.
■12. to *use* words to *exchange minimal information with an adult*. (Child initiates conversation; requests or questions not applicable.)
Examples:
   a. *During milk and cookie time, child says, "My mommy makes cookies."*
   b. *Child says to teacher, "This is a red crayon."*
   c. *Child says, "I want to go home."*
■13. to *use* words spontaneously to *exchange minimal information with another child*. (Minimal verbal spontaneity with information content; requests or questions are not applicable.)
   Self-explanatory

Socialization Objectives

STAGE I:
Responding to the Environment with Pleasure

STAGE I SOCIALIZATION GOAL: *TO TRUST AN ADULT SUFFICIENTLY TO RESPOND TO HIM*

■ 1.   to be *aware* of others. (Child looks at adult or another child when adult or another child speaks directly to child or touches him.)
Examples:
   a.   Child is sitting at the table staring at the wall. Teacher calls child by name and touches child on the back. Then child turns head toward adult. (Child may not be responding to his name as much as to the physical contact from the teacher.)
   b.   Child is aimlessly wandering around the room. Teacher puts her arm around the child and says child's name. Child turns head away from adult. (Child is obviously aware of the contact from the adult but resists looking at the adult.)
   c.   Child shows awareness of others by body language or averted gaze but not necessarily by eye contact.
   d.   Child shows some interest in baby games such as peek-a-boo.
■ 2.   to *attend* to other's behavior. (Child looks at another when attention is not on child directly.)
Example:
   Teacher is giving help to child. Second child watches the teacher and child together.
■ 3.   to *respond* to adult when child's name is called. (Child looks at adult or away; appropriate or inappropriate response acceptable.)
Example:
   Teacher calls child's name. Child looks up or around to teacher. (In this objective, child does not need to be physically aroused, as in socialization objective S-1. Child differentiates his own name from other children's names. He may look away, instead of toward teacher, when name is called.)
■ 4.   Child *interacts nonverbally* with *adult* to meet needs.
Examples:
   a.   Child moves adult's hand to get cookie.
   b.   Child points to desired object.
   c.   Teacher turns on toy radio. Radio winds down. Child comes to adult to turn it on again.
   d.   Child tries to bite teacher's arm after a frustrating experience.
■ 5.   to engage in *organized solitary play* (with direction from adult if necessary; age-appropriate play not necessary).
Examples:
   a.   Child purposefully piles blocks together, knocks them down, repeats, or builds a house. Teacher may initiate activity by stacking blocks as example and saying, "Let's stack the blocks."
   b.   Child climbs up and down the slide.
   c.   Child puts toys in box, then dumps them out.
   d.   Patterned play.
■ 6.   to respond to adult's verbal and nonverbal *requests to come* to him. (Child moves next to adult and looks at him, and child accepts adult's touch.)
Examples:
   a.   Teacher says, "Come over here by me." Child moves next to teacher and allows teacher to put arm around him.
   b.   During story time on floor, teacher holds arm out to child to get him to move next to her. Child moves over by teacher and looks at her.
■ 7.   to demonstrate *understanding* of *single verbal requests* or directions given directly to child. (Adult does not use gestures.)
Example:
   Teacher says, "Sit down." Child sits down. Teacher says, "Hang up your coat." Child hangs up coat without physical intervention.
   "Put the ball in the cabinet."
   "Pick up the truck."   } *Child complies.*
   "Give me the box."
■ 8.   to produce a *recognizable single word or sign* in several activities to obtain a *desired response from adult* or to label for adult (e.g., "water" instead of "wa-wa" for water). (Verbal cues may be used.)
■ 9.   to produce *recognizable single words or signs* in several activities to obtain a *desired response from another child* or to label for child. (Verbal cues may be used.)
Examples:
   a.   At play time, child sees another child with his favorite truck. He walks up and says or signs, "Truck."
   b.   Child A tries to sit in child B's chair. B begins to get upset. Teacher says, "Tell him to move." B says or signs, "Move."
■10.   to produce a *meaningful*, recognizable *sequence of words or signs* in several activities (without a model) to obtain a desired response from *others* or to label for others. (Gestures or verbal cues may be used.)
Examples:
   a.   Child says (or signs), "Go away."
   b.   Child says (or signs), "Big fire truck."

■11. to exhibit a *beginning* emergence *of self* (indicated by any of these: age-approximate human figure drawing; gesturing pleasure at one's work; use of personal pronoun (I, me, my); or looking at self in mirror).

Examples:
  a. *Child looks at self in mirror; child does not avoid it.*
  b. *Child uses personal pronoun but may not be grammatically correct ("Me going," or "Me toy").*
  c. *Child takes his drawing up to teacher with smile and conveys pride in work.*

■12. to *seek* contact with adult *spontaneously*. (Child moves next to adult or touches him.)

Examples:
  a. *Child walks into room at beginning of class and comes to teacher for a hug.*
  b. *During play time, child moves next to teacher and strokes her hair.*

STAGE II:
Responding to the Environment with Success

STAGE II SOCIALIZATION GOAL: *TO PARTICIPATE IN ACTIVITIES WITH OTHERS*

■13. to *participate spontaneously* in specific parallel activities near another child using similar materials but not interacting.
Example:
> *Child plays with toy truck while another child is using a car. They are organized individually, i.e., each runs on his own highway, and "traffic" of other child serves as no impetus for interaction.*

■14. *to wait* without physical intervention by adults. (Verbal support or touch may be used.) (Same as behavior objective B-9.)
Examples:
> a. *Child races up to roll on the mats but is out of turn. Teacher says, "Wow, you are really happy about having mat time! I can't wait to see how well you do your cartwheel after Ricky finishes." Child goes in turn.*
> b. *Mike wants the cookies, and he wants them NOW. Teacher says, "You can have a cookie after John." Mike is able to wait.*
> c. *Child wants his turn first at kickball. Teacher says, "I remember that fly ball you caught yesterday. You were standing right here." Or, "Everyone gets a chance to kick and catch. It's your turn to catch now." Child moves to field.*
> d. *Child runs out of the room ahead of the group. Teacher says, "Wait at the door." Child waits.*

■15. to *initiate* appropriate minimal movement toward another child within the classroom routine. (Child, through gesture and action, begins minimal appropriate social interaction with another child.)
Examples:
> a. *Child remembers that another child missed his turn.*
> b. *Child wants to sit by a certain child.*
> c. *Child goes over to join another child already engaged in play.*

■16. to *participate* in a verbally directed sharing activity. (Child passes materials or gives toy to another.)
Examples:
> a. *Child passes cookies within the classroom structure.*
> b. *Child gives toy to another. (Verbal cues may be used.)*
> c. *Child can use same paint, water, or box of crayons that another child is using.*

■17. to *participate* in cooperative activities or projects with another child during play time, indoor or outdoor. (Child is involved actively with another child; verbal support or touch may be used.)
Examples:
> *(Involvement in a free-play situation or organized game where a child is able to organize his play and allow for successful interaction with another child in the group.)*
> a. *Child attends a "tea party" with other children.*
> b. *Child puts out "fire" at another child's "home."*
> c. *Child stays in circle and plays "drop the hankie" following structure of group's game.*

■18. to *participate* in cooperative activities or projects with another child during organized class activities. (Child is involved actively with others; verbal support or touch may be used.)
Examples:
> *(The child engages in activities that the teacher directs by determining the procedure that will guide the children toward desired outcomes, products, etc.)*
> a. *Child has a defined place on a large piece of paper for a group mural on which each child has a specific area to complete.*
> b. *Child role plays a story book character as other children serve as audience.*
> c. *Child makes cold drink mix with another child.*

Academic Objectives

STAGE I:
Responding to the Environment with Pleasure

STAGE I ACADEMIC GOAL: *TO RESPOND TO THE ENVIRONMENT WITH PROCESSES OF CLASSIFICATION, DISCRIMINATION, BASIC RECEPTIVE LANGUAGE, AND BODY COORDINATION*

■ 1. to *react* to sensory stimulus by *attending* toward source of stimulus by body response or by looking (in situations using tactile, motor, visual, auditory, taste, or smell stimuli). (Same as behavior objective B-1.) Child must have two out of six modalities.

Examples:
   a. *After teacher blows bubbles, child attends briefly by looking or responding with body language (visual stimulus).*
   b. *When teacher starts to play guitar, child attends briefly by turning head to source of sound, looking at guitar or teacher, or smiling (auditory stimulus).*
   c. *When teacher places child's hand in water, child indicates awareness by splashing or clapping hands together, withdrawing hands, or looking briefly at water (tactile stimulus).*

■ 2. to *respond* to stimulus by *sustained attending* toward source of stimulus (continued looking at object or person after initial stimulus-response has occurred). (Same as behavior objective B-2)

Examples:
   a. *After initial stimulus, child continues to watch teacher strum guitar during a song or continues to smile or move body to music.*
   b. *Child continues to look at or play in water.*

■ 3. to *respond* spontaneously to *single* environmental *stimulus* with a motor behavior: object, person, sound. (Same as behavior objective B-3.)

Examples:
   a. *Child sees block, picks it up, and throws it.*
   b. *Teacher holds out guitar. Child explores it.*
   c. *Teacher turns on music box (out of child's view). Child comes to see.*

■ 4. to respond with motor and body responses to *complex* environmental and verbal *stimuli* (through imitation "Do this;" through completion of verbal direction; or through minimal participation in activities) *given physical intervention and verbal cues.* (Same as behavior objective B-4.)

Examples:
   a. *Parent says, "It's time to play in the water." Parent puts her hands in the water and splashes (to show child what to do). Then child puts hands in the water and splashes.*
   b. *Teacher says, "This is a boat. Let's push it." Teacher pushes boat as example. Child does not respond, so teacher places child's hand on boat. Then child begins to play with boat. Teacher says, "Good, you're playing with the boat" and pats child on the back.*
   c. *Teacher announces, "It's play time." Child gets up but is not sure in which direction to move. Teacher steers child (with hand on back) to play area. Child sits down in play area but doesn't initiate play, so teacher hands child a toy. Child takes toy.*

■ 5. to respond with rudimentary *fine* and *gross motor skills* to simple manipulative tasks associated with *24-month* age level. Child must have mastered two skills in each area in order to master this objective.

Fine Motor Examples:
   a. *Child can build tower of six to seven blocks.*
   b. *Child can align two or more blocks together to make a train.*
   c. *Child imitates circular stroke and vertical stroke.*
   d. *Child can maintain spoon in upright position.*
   e. *Child can pull on or take off a simple garmet (shoes, socks, or panties).*
   f. *Child turns knob (door knob or jar lid).*

Gross Motor Examples:
   a. *Child can walk unassisted.*
   b. *Child can run.*
   c. *Child can climb.*
   d. *Child can kick a ball.*

■ 6. to *imitate* simple, familiar *actions* of *adult.*

Examples:
   a. *Teacher says, "Bye-bye" and waves. Child waves.*
   b. *Teacher bounces ball then gives ball to child. Child attempts to bounce ball.*
   c. *Teacher stacks up blocks and knocks them down. Teacher pushes blocks to child. Child imitates.*

■ 7. to respond by *simple discrimination* of objects. (Child gives correct motor or verbal response to a command such as, "Give me ____." Or, "Touch the ____." (Two different objects presented.)
Example:
> *Teacher puts crayons and scissors on table and says to child, "Give me the crayons." Child can discriminate between the two objects and hands the correct item to teacher.*

■ 8. to *respond* to question by naming single object with a *recognizable approximation* of the *appropriate verbal response*. (Child gives approximation, by word or sign, to question, "What is this?" Object present; function or name acceptable.)

■ 9. to *voluntarily* use *recognizable single word approximations* in several activities to describe or label a situation, object, or event. (Child produces recognizable approximation spontaneously, e.g., "wa-wa" for water.) (Same as communication objective C-4.)
Examples:
> a. *Parent puts milk on the table, and child spontaneously says, "Mi, mi."*
> b. *Teacher blows bubbles, saying, "I have bubbles, bubbles." As teacher begins blowing bubbles again, child excitedly attempts to say, "Bu, bu."*
> c. *Child sees car going down street. Child says, "Ca."*
> d. *Teacher is hopping, encouraging children to model. She is saying, "Hop-hop-hop." Suddenly child says, "Op, op."*

■10. to demonstrate short term *memory* for sound patterns, objects, or people.
Examples:
> a. *For sounds, by repeating simple sound patterns.*
> b. *For objects, by searching for hidden objects.*
> c. *For people, by indicating awareness of their absence.*

■11. to match *similar objects* with *different attributes*. Visual matching of concrete objects having same attributes. Adult should provide a verbal direction while presenting this task: "Find one that's the same." Or, "Let's put all the trucks here." Child does not need to understand verbal direction.
Examples:
> a. *Child fits geometric blocks into puzzle box opening without using trial-and-error method.*
> b. *Child can do simple (single pieces) puzzle, fitting shapes into matching spaces.*
> c. *Child is presented with red and blue beads. Teacher demonstrates putting red beads in one box and blue in another. Child continues task.*
> d. *At play time, child gets several different trucks and puts them in one place together.*

■12. to produce *recognizable single words* to *label* simple pictures or objects (spontaneously or elicited). No models given.

■13. to perform *body coordination* activities at the three/four-year level. Child must master at least two skills in order to master objective.
Examples:
> a. *Child can ride a tricycle.*
> b. *Child can alternate feet when going up stairs.*
> c. *Child can stand balanced on one foot.*
> d. *Child can catch bounced ball.*
> e. *Child can throw ball, two hands overhead.*
> f. *Child can jump forward.*

■14. to *match identical pictures* when presented with both identical and different pictures. (Adult should provide a verbal direction while presenting the task, "Find one that's the same," or comparable statement. Child must understand verbal direction.)

■15. to recognize several *body parts (eye, hand, foot, nose, leg, arm, knee).* (Any correct response acceptable: gesture, word, etc.)

■16. to perform *fine motor* coordination activities at the *three/four-year* level. Child must master at least two skills in order to master objective.
Examples:
> a. *Child builds a bridge from cubes.*
> b. *Child copies a circle.*
> c. *Child draws man with two parts.*
> d. *Child buttons and unbuttons.*
> e. *Child strings beads.*
> f. *Child snips with scissors.*

■17. to recognize several *colors.* (Any correct response acceptable: gesture, word, etc.)

STAGE II:
Responding to the Environment with Success

STAGE II ACADEMIC GOAL: *TO PARTICIPATE IN CLASSROOM ACTIVITIES WITH LANGUAGE CONCEPTS OF SIMILARITIES AND DIFFERENCES, LABELS, USE, COLOR; NUMERICAL PROCESSES OF ORDERING AND CLASSIFYING; AND BODY COORDINATION*

■18. to recognize *uses* of several objects or toys.
Examples:
    a. *Teacher has object or picture of object, like a shovel. Child knows what it is used for and can tell or act it out.*
    b. *Teacher hands ball and says, "What can you do with this?" Child says or acts it out by throwing, kicking, bouncing, or rolling it.*

■19. to recognize *detail in pictures* by gesture or word.
Example:
    Teacher says, "Where's the girl in the picture?" "Where's her nose?" Child points or describes correctly.

■20. to recognize *one different object* in a set of three objects. Adult should provide a verbal direction while presenting this task: "Find the one that's different." Or, "Which one doesn't belong?" Child must understand verbal direction.
Examples:
    a. *Teacher presents box with two identical trucks and one doll. Teacher says, "Find one that doesn't belong."*
    b. *Teacher presents two spoons and one fork. Teacher says, "Which one is different?"*

■21. to *count* with *one-to-one* correspondence to *five*.
Example:
    Child can count five objects.

■22. to recognize *pictures* that are the same and ones that are different. Child must understand adult's directions: "Find the one that's the same," "Find the one that's different," or comparable statement.
Example:
    Child is presented with three pictures. Two are identical; one is different. Teacher says, "Show me the one that's different." After child identifies picture that is different, teacher removes the two identical pictures and adds another picture making the different picture one of two now the same. A third, different, picture is added. Teacher says, "Now, find the ones that are the same." (Teacher needs two different sets of identical pairs and one different card for this task.)

■23. to *count* with *one-to-one* correspondence to *ten*.
Example:
    Child can count ten objects.

■24. to perform *eye-hand coordination* activities at the *five-year level*.
Examples:
    a. *Child draws a recognizable person with body.*
    b. *Child copies triangle, rectangle.*
    c. *Child prints a few letters from memory.*
    d. *Child copies first name from model.*
    e. *Child draws simple house representation.*
    f. *Child cuts with scissors along lines.*

■25. to recognize symbols, numerals, and written words that are the *same* and ones that are *different*. (All forms must be mastered; child need not know how to read words in order to recognize differences among them but must understand verbal directions.)
Example:
    Teacher shows child a card with several words, two identical and one different. Teacher asks, "Which one is different?" "Now, which ones are the same?"

■26. to *categorize* simple *pictures* that are *different but have* generally *similar characteristics* or associations.
Examples:
    a. *Teacher gives child a stack of picture cards and says, "Put all the people in this pile and put all the animals in this pile."*
    b. *Teacher prepares worksheet for child and says, "Draw a line to the pictures that belong together." (Sheet contains pictures of chicken and egg, dog and bone, pencil and paper, paint and brush.)*

■27. to *write* a *recognizable approximation* of *first name* without assistance. (Adult may initiate request; no model used.)
    Self explanatory

■28. to *discriminate* concepts of *differences* in *up, down; under, over; big, little; tall, small; hot, cold; first, last.*
    Self explanatory

■29. to perform *body coordination* activities at the *five-year level.*

Examples:
    a. *Child skips, using alternate feet.*
    b. *Child walks on walking board.*
■30. to *recognize groups* of objects to *five* ("How many?").
Example:
    Teacher holds up card with dots for brief viewing. Child identifies number without counting.
■31. to *listen* to storytelling.
Example:
    Child can direct and maintain attention to the story being told or read by the teacher. (Verbal support or touch may be used.)

appendix b
DEVELOPMENTAL THERAPY OBJECTIVES RATING FORM

The Developmental Therapy curriculum objectives are used with a rating form (DTORF) which contains abbreviated statements of each of the objectives that a child has and has not mastered. Objectives should be selected in the order in which they occur on the rating form, at least one X (indicating that a child is ready to begin or needs to continue intensive work on the objective) but no more than four in each curriuclum area at any given time. The objectives not mastered become the major therapy for the child.

For basic instructions in using the DTORF see Chapter 2 of *Developmental Therapy* (edited by Mary M. Wood), "Developmental Therapy Curriculum Objectives," by Carolyn Combs.

Photograph by Larry White, Athens Newspaper, Inc., Athens, Georgia

Child's Name _____ Class Stage _____ Raters: _____

Date _____ Type Rating (Check one)—Baseline _____ , 5th week _____ , 10th week _____

Behavior	Communication	Socialization	(Pre)Academics

STAGE I

Behavior	Communication	Socialization	(Pre)Academics
___ 0. indicate awareness	___ 0. produce sounds	___ 1. aware/others	___ 1. same as B-1
___ tactile	___ 1. attend speaker	___ 2. attend/others beh.	___ 2. same as B-2
___ auditory	___ 2. resp. verb. stim./mot. beh.	___ 3. resp. to name	___ 3. same as B-3
___ motor	___ 3. resp./verbal approx.	___ 4. interact/adult nonverb.	___ 4. same as B-4
___ taste	___ 4. wrd. approx./descr./label/volunt.	___ 5. solit. play	___ 5. fine/gross mot./24 mo.
___ visual	___ 5. recog. word/to adult	___ 6. resp. request/come	___ 6. imitate acts of adults
___ smell	___ 6. recog. word/to child	___ 7. dem. under./sing. req.	___ 7. discrim. of obj.
___ 1. react by attending	___ 7. word sequence	___ 8. recog. wd./sign adult	___ 8. approx. naming object
___ 2. respond by sust. attend.		___ 9. recog. wd./sign child	___ 9. same as C-4
___ 3. simp. stim/motor behav.		___ 10. word seqs/others	___ 10. short term memory/sound, obj. & people.
___ 4. complex stim./imit.		___ 11. begin. emerg./self	___ 11. match simil. obj. w/diff. attri.
___ 5. assist in self help		___ 12. contact/adult spont.	___ 12. wrd./label pic., obj.
___ 6. respond indep./play mat.			___ 13. body coord./3-4 yr. level
___ 7. indicate recall of routine			___ 14. match identical pic.
			___ 15. recog. body parts
			___ 16. fine motor coord./3-4 yr.
			___ 17. recog. colors

STAGE II

Behavior	Communication	Socialization	(Pre)Academics
___ 8. use play mat. appro.	___ 8. answer/recog. word	___ 13. parallel activ.	___ 18. recog. use of obj.
___ 9. to wait/no interven.	___ 9. recept. vocab./2	___ 14. same as B-9	___ 19. recog. detail in pictures
___ 10. particip./sitting no interven.	___ 10. label feel./pict.	___ 15. init. min. move./child	___ 20. recog. diff. obj.
___ 11. particip./movement no interven.	___ 11. command, request/simple wrd. seq.	___ 16. sharing activ.	___ 21. count to 5 (1 to 1)
___ 12. spon. particip./activ.	___ 12. use words ex. min. info./adult	___ 17. coop. act./child at play	___ 22. recog. same/diff. pictures
	___ 13. use words ex. min. info./child	___ 18. coop. act./child in organ. activ.	___ 23. count to 10 (1 to 1)
			___ 24. eye-hand coord./5-yr. level
			___ 25. recog./shapes, symbols, numerals, words/same/diff.
			___ 26. categorize diff. pictures/similar charac.
			___ 27. write recog. approx. of first name w/o asst.
			___ 28. discrim. differences (up-down, etc.)
			___ 29. body coord./5-yr. lev.
			___ 30. recog. grps. to 5
			___ 31. listen to storytelling

STAGE III

Behavior	Communication	Socialization	(Pre)Academics
___ 13. vb. recall rules/proced.	___ 14. accept praise	___ 19. turns w/o remind.	___ 32. recog. grps. to 10
___ 14. contrib. to grp. expect.	___ 15. same as B-13	___ 20. share/min. remind.	___ 33. left-right visual orien.
___ 15. vb. conseq./expect.	___ 16. spon. describe work	___ 21. sug. to teacher	___ 34. recog. writ. names for color words
___ 16. vb. reasons/expect.	___ 17. same as B-14	___ 22. partic./act. suggest child	___ 35. recog. written labels
___ 17. vb. other ways beh./indiv.	___ 18. same as B-15	___ 23. pref./child	___ 36. recog. & write numerals for groups/1-10
___ 18. refrain when others	___ 19. pride/words/gestures	___ 24. desc. charac. of others	___ 37. write first/last name/date with sample
___ 19. main. control & comply	___ 20. vb./feeling/resp.		___ 38. eye-hand coord./6-yr. level
	___ 21. same as B-16		___ 39. body-coord./6-yr. level
			___ 40. recog. & write numerals for grps./11-20
			___ 41. write alpha./simple words

(continued)

	Behavior	Communication	Socialization	(Pre)Academics
STAGE III				___ 42. do add-subtract thru 10 ___ 43. use ordinal concepts verbally ___ 44. lstn. to story & resp. appro. ___ 45. read prim. vocab./sentences ___ 46. add-subtract above 10 ___ 47. write basic words/memory or dictation ___ 48. partic. grp. act./write, tell, mural
STAGE IV	___ 20. resp. appro./leader choice ___ 21. spon. partic./activ. prev. avoid ___ 22. implem. alter. beh. ___ 23. vb. express cause & ef. ___ 24. resp./provocation/ control ___ 25. resp. appro./ new suggest.	___ 22. vb. recog. feel/others ___ 23. vb. recog. feel/self ___ 24. verb. praise/others ___ 25. non vb./express./ feel./art, music ___ 26. spon. express. own feel./words ___ 27. express others feel. ___ 28. vb. express. exper./ feel./art, music ___ 29. same as B-23	___ 25. suggest. act./grp. ___ 26. same as B-20 ___ 27. same as B-21 ___ 28. diff. charac./others ___ 29. phys./vb. support/ others ___ 30. partic. grp. plng. & pb. solv.	___ 49. write name, ad., date/memory ___ 50. read, write/sentences ___ 51. read, write quant. words ___ 52. contribute grp. project/ expressive skills ___ 53. write indiv. exper. stories
STAGE V	___ 26. construc. suggest.	___ 30. maintain posit. relats. verb.	___ 31. init. & main./ interp. & grp. rel.	___ 54. write for commun. ___ 55. read/pleas. & info. ___ 56. write of feel. & attit. ___ 57. read/info. feel. & beh. of others

Progress Notes

FORMAT FOR AN INDIVIDUALIZED EDUCATION PROGRAM (IEP)

A developmentally oriented approach to planning Individualized Education Programs (IEP) has been designed by the staff at the Rutland Center in Athens, Georgia. The Rutland Center — Developmental Therapy IEP format has two parts: one that is completed by the professional staff and shared with parents following the intake-diagnostic process, and one that is used after a child is enrolled in a Developmental Therapy class.

Part I includes information on how the child is currently functioning, the severity of his problem, and long and short term recommendations for school programs, parent participation, and treatment-oriented goals. This part is used as a format for reporting the results of a child's evaluation and as a means of reaching decisions with parents about the best courses of action to meet their child's individual needs.

Part II of the form focuses on short and long term educational goals. Using the Developmental Therapy objectives, parents and teacher-therapists formulate short term objectives in the areas of Behavior, Communication, Socialization, and (Pre)Academics and decide upon materials and techniques that will be used to reach these goals.

Photograph by Larry White, Athens Newspaper, Inc., Athens, Georgia

Rutland Center — Developmental Therapy
Individualized Education Program (IEP)

PART I

STAFFING REPORT

AND LONG TERM RECOMMENDATIONS

CHILD _____ ID No. _____

Date of Staffing _____/_____/_____

Names of Persons Completing this Section (three of five must participate)

_____ , Psychologist

_____ , Psychiatrist

_____ , Educational Diagnostician

_____ , Social Worker

_____ , Other, Specify position

_____

Signature of parent or legal
guardian indicating that this
IEP Part I Information has
been discussed and approved.

Date _____

Signature of staff person
responsible for coordinating
diagnostic services

IEP for _____

Rutland Center — Developmental Therapy
Individualized Education Program (IEP)

TO BE COMPLETED PRIOR TO STAFFING	TO BE COMPLETED AT STAFFING

Name _____

Date of Birth _____

Age _____

Referral Source_____

School_____Grade _____

Teacher _____

Principal _____

Accepted: Yes_____No_____

Parent Planning Conference _____

   (Name staff person) _____

Planning Conference with School _____

   (Name staff person)_____

Recommended School and Parent Meet

   Together?   Yes_____No _____

INTAKE CONTACTS

	Examiner	Date
PSYCHOLOGICAL		
EDUCATIONAL		
PSYCHIATRIC		
PARENT CONFERENCES		
SCHOOL CONTACT		
(name:		)

SUMMARY — View of Problem

	Level of Problem					
	none	mild			severe	
BEHAVIOR	0	1	2	3	4	5
COMMUNICATION	0	1	2	3	4	5
SOCIALIZATION	0	1	2	3	4	5
(PRE)ACADEMICS	0	1	2	3	4	5
OVERALL	0	1	2	3	4	5

Present Stages of Child's Development

Behavior_____

Communication_____

Socialization _____

Academics _____

Recommended Developmental Therapy Placement: (to be completed only for children accepted)

Projected Enrollment Date _____

Stage _____

Time _____

Team _____

Long Term Goals:

Projected Terminating Date_____

Projected Terminating Stage _____

Major Problems (RFCL & Other)

Home

School

Intake Staff

Recommendations for Major Home Focus:

Recommended Level of   Minimal   _____
Parental Participation: Intermittent   _____
   Check One   Extensive   _____   Parent Worker _____

Type and Amount of Regular Educational Programs and School Experiences Needed:

Staff Person for School Liaison: _____

Recommendations for Other Support Services:

Medical/Diagnostics/Medication Needed:

Staff Person: _____

Rutland Center — Developmental Therapy
Individualized Education Program (IEP)

PART II

Child _____

Name of Persons Completing this Section

_____ , Parent or Guardian

_____ , Lead Teacher

_____ , Support Teacher

_____ , Parent Worker

_____ , Others

_____

Signature of parent or guardian
indicating that this IEP has been
developed with parental (or guardian)
assistance and endorsement

Date _____

IEP for _____

TO BE COMPLETED ON THE 8TH DAY OF PARTICIPATION
OR DURING THE SCHOOL YEAR
BY TREATMENT TEAM AND PARENT

1. Evaluation of child's present level of performance and annual progress record.
   (Attach the Developmental Therapy Objectives Rating Form Summary.)

2. <u>Short Term Objectives</u>: (__Baseline,__Week) <u>Suggested Methods, Materials, and</u>
   <u>Experiences</u>:

<u>BEHAVIOR</u>

<u>COMMUNICATION</u>

IEP for _____

(CONTINUED)

2. <u>Short Term Objectives</u>: (___Baseline, ___Week) <u>Suggested Methods, Materials, and
Experiences</u>:

<u>SOCIALIZATION</u>

<u>(PRE)ACADEMICS</u>

IEP for _____

MAJOR PROGRAM CHANGES:

Date _____

_____
Signature of parent or guardian
indicating that this information
has been discussed and approved
Date _____

Date _____

_____
Signature of staff person
responsible for coordinating
program changes

_____
Signature of parent or guardian
indicating that this information
has been discussed and approved
Date _____

Date _____

_____
Signature of staff person
responsible for coordinating
program changes

_____
Signature of parent or guardian
indicating that this information
has been discussed and approved
Date _____

Date _____

_____
Signature of staff person
responsible for coordinating
program changes

_____
Signature of parent or guardian
indicating that this information
has been discussed and approved
Date _____

_____
Signature of staff person
responsible for coordinating
program changes

IEP for _____

Recomendations for End of the School Year:

_____   _____
Signature of parent or guardian   Signature of staff person
indicating that this information   responsible for coordinating
has been discussed and approved   end of year planning
Date _____

Proposed Recommendations at Termination and for Follow-up:

Date of Termination _____   Date of Parent Conference and Termination
_____ , Lead Teacher   RFCL _____
_____ , Support Teacher   Date of Teacher Conference and Termination
_____ , Parent Worker   RFCL _____
_____ , Other

_____   _____
Signature of parent or guardian   Signature of staff person
indicating that this information   responsible for coordinating
has been discussed and approved   termination
Date _____

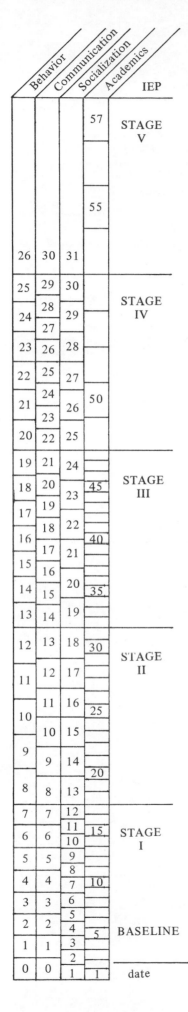

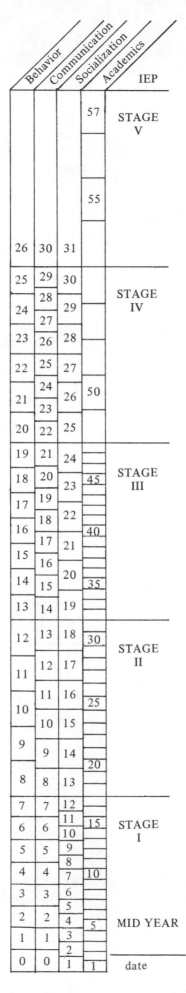

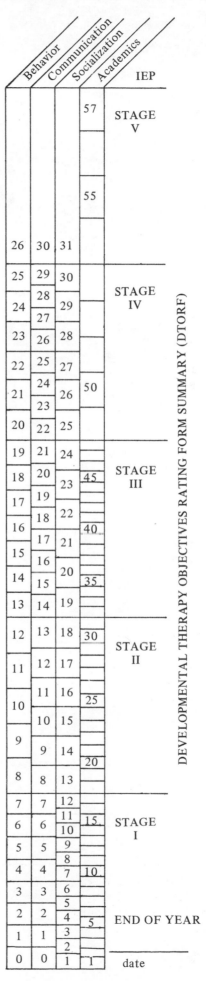

DEVELOPMENTAL THERAPY OBJECTIVES RATING FORM SUMMARY (DTORF)

Mark objectives mastered in yellow.
Mark current objectives in pencil.
Objectives "not yet ready" should be left unmarked.

CHILD _____

SUGGESTED READINGS

Photograph by Larry White, Athens Newspaper, Inc., Athens, Georgia

Adler, J. 1973. Looking for Me. (16 mm film). University of California, Berkeley, Cal.

Anthony, E. J. 1956. The significance of Jean Piaget for child psychiatry. Br. J. Med. Psychol. 29:20–34.

Arena, J. I. 1969. Teaching Through Sensory-motor Experiences. Academic Therapy Publications, San Rafael, Cal.

Ayres, J. A. 1975. Sensory Integration and Learning Disorders. Western Psychological Services, Los Angeles.

Bandura, A. 1962. Social learning through imitation. In M. R. Jones (ed.), Nebraska Symposium on Motivation, pp. 211–269. University of Nebraska Press, Lincoln.

Bandura, A. 1969. Social-learning theory of identificatory process. In D. A. Goslin (ed.), Handbook of Socialization Theory and Research, pp. 213–262. Rand McNally & Company, Chicago.

Bell, S. M. 1970. The development of the concept of the object and its relationship to infant-mother attachment. Child Dev. 41:291–312.

Beller, E. K. 1955. Dependency and independence in young children. J. Genet. Psychol. 87:25–35.

Bender, L. 1968. Childhood schizophrenia: A review. Int. J. Psychiatry 5:211–220.

Biber, B., and Franklin, M. 1967. The relevance of developmental and pschodynamic concepts to the education of the preschool child. J. Am. Acad. Child Psychiatry 6:5–24.

Bobroff, A. 1960. The stages of maturation in socialized thinking and in the ego development of two groups of children. Child Dev. 31:321–338.

Bricker, W. A., and Bricker, D. 1974. An early language training strategy. In R. L. Schiefelbusch and L. L. Lloyd (eds.), Language perspectives—Acquisition, Retardation, and Intervention, pp. 431–468. University Park Press, Baltimore.

Bruner, J. S. 1959. The cognitive consequences of early sensory deprivation. Psychosom. Med. 21:89–95.

Bruner, J. S. 1966. On cognitive growth. In J. Bruner, R. Oliver, and P. Greenfield (eds.), Studies in Cognitive Growth, pp. 1–67. John Wiley & Sons, Inc., New York.

Cazden, C. B. 1972. Child Language and Education. Holt, Rinehart, and Winston, Inc., New York.

Coffey, H., and Wiener, L. 1967. Group Treatment of Autistic Children. Prentice-Hall Inc., Englewood Cliffs, N. J.

Combs, C. 1975. Developmental therapy curriculum objectives. In M. M. Wood (ed.), Developmental Therapy, pp. 17–35. University Park Press, Baltimore.

Creak, M. 1964. Schizophrenic syndrome in childhood. Further progress report of a working party. Dev. Med. Child Neurol. 4:530–535.

Deslauriers, A. M., and Carlson, C. F. 1969. Your Child is Asleep: Early Infantile Autism. Dorsey Press, Homewood, Ill.

Dubnoff, B. 1965. The habitation and education of the autistic child in a therapeutic day school. J. School Psychol. 4:52–59.

Ekstein, R., and Caruth, E. 1976. On the structure of inner and outer spielraum—the play space of the schizophrenic child. In E. Schopler and R. J. Reichler (eds.), Psychopathology and Child Development. pp. 311–318 Plenum Press Inc., New York

Elkind, D. 1967. Piaget and Montessori. Harvard Ed. Rev. 37:535–545.

Elkind, D. 1976. Cognitive development and psychopathology: Observations on egocentrism and ego defense. In E. Schopler and R. J. Reichler (eds.), Psychopathology and Child Development, pp. 168–183. Plenum Press Inc., New York.

Erikson, E. H. 1963. Childhood and Society. 2nd Ed. W. W. Norton & Company Inc., New York.

Fenichel, C. 1971. Psycho-educational approaches for seriously disturbed children in the classroom. In N. J. Long, W. C. Morse, and R. G. Newman (eds.), Conflict in the Classroom, 2nd ed., pp. 337–345. Wadsworth Publishing Company Inc., Belmont, Cal.

Ferster, C. B., and DeMyer, M. K. 1964. The development of performances in autistic children in an automatically controlled environment. In H. J. Eysenck (ed.), Experiments in Behavior Therapy, pp. 509–545. The Macmillan Company, New York.

Flavell, J. H. 1963. The Developmental Psychology of Jean Piaget. D. Van Nostrand Company Inc., Princeton, N.J.

Flavell, J. 1972. An analysis of cognitive developmental sequences. Genet. Psychol. Monogr. 86:279–350.

Freud, A. 1957. Ego and the Mechanisms of Defence. Hogarth Press Ltd., London.

Gesell, A. 1974. Infant and Child in the Culture of Today. Harper & Row, New York.

Gesell, A. 1975. Developmental Diagnosis. 3rd Ed. H. Knoblock and B. Panamanick (eds.). Harper & Row, New York. (particularly chapters 14, 15, and 16)

Gottman, J., Gonso, J., and Schuler, P. 1976. Teaching social skills to isolated children. J. Abnorm. Child Psychol. 4:179–197.

Gray, S. W., Klaus, R. A., Miller, J. O., and Forrester, B. J. 1966. Before First Grade. Teachers College Press, New York.

Hartup, W. W. 1963. Dependence and independence. In

H. W. Stevenson (ed.), Child Psychology, Nat. Soc. for Study of Educ. Yearbook, Pt. 1, pp. 333–363. Chicago University Press, Chicago.

Hellmuth, J. (ed.). 1967. The Exceptional Infant. Vols. 1 and 2. Brunner/Mazel Publishers, New York.

Herbert, M. 1974. Emotional Problems of Development in Children. Academic Press Inc., New York.

Hermelin, B. 1966. Psychological research. In J. K. Wing (ed.), Childhood Autism: Clinical, Educational and Social Aspects, pp. 159–173. Pergamon Press Ltd., Oxford.

Hermelin, B., and Frith, U. 1971. Psychological studies of childhood autism: Can autistic children make sense of what they see and hear? J. Spec. Educ. 5:107–117.

Hermelin, B., and O'Conner, N. 1970. Psychological Experiments with Autistic Children. Pergamon Press Inc., New York.

Hewett, F. 1968. The Emotionally Disturbed Child in the Classroom. Allyn & Bacon, Rockleigh, N.J.

Hewett, F. 1975. Education of Exceptional Learners. Allyn & Bacon, Rockleigh, N. J.

Huberty, C. J., Quirk, J. P., and Swan, W. W. 1973. An evaluation system for a psychoeducational treatment program for emotionally disturbed children. Educ. Technol. May:73–82.

Huberty, C. J., and Swan, W. W. 1975. Evaluation of programs. In J. Jordon, A. Hayden, M. Karnes, and M. M. Wood (eds.), Early Childhood Education for Exceptional Children—A Handbook of Ideas and Exemplary Practices. Council for Exceptional Children, Reston, Va.

Ilg, F. L. and Ames, L. B. 1965. School Readiness. Harper & Row, New York.

Inhelder, B. 1957. Developmental psychology. Annu. Rev. Psychol. 8:139–162.

Kagan, J. 1958. The concept of identification. Psychol. Rev. 65:296–305.

Kagan, J. 1971. Change and Continuity in Infancy. John Wiley & Sons Inc., New York.

Kagan, J., and Moss, H. 1962. Birth to Maturity: A Study in Psychological Development. John Wiley & Sons Inc., New York.

Kanner, L. 1943. Autistic disturbances of affective contact. Nervous Child 2:216–250.

Kaufman, B. N. 1976. Son Rise. Harper & Row, New York.

Keister, M. 1938. The behavior of young children in failure: An experimental attempt to discover and to modify undesirable responses of preschool children to failure. University of Iowa Studies in Child Welfare 14:27–82.

Kliman, G. 1971. Psychological Emergencies of Childhood. Grune & Stratton Inc., New York.

Kohlberg, L. 1968. Early education: A cognitive-developmental view. Child Dev. 39:1013–1062.

Kuglemass, I. N. 1970. The Autistic Child. Charles C Thomas, Springfield, Ill.

Lotter, V. 1967. Epidemiology of autistic conditions in young children: II. Some characteristics of the parents and children. Soc. Psychiatry 1:163–173.

Luria, A. R. 1961. The Role of Speech in the Regulation of Normal and Abnormal Behaviour. Pergamon Press Ltd., Oxford.

Mahler, M. S. 1952. On childhood psychoses and schizophrenia: Autistic and symbiotic infantile psychoses. Psychoanal. Study Child 7:286–305.

Mattick, I., and Murphy, Z. B. 1971. Cognitive disturbances in young children. In J. Hellmuth (ed.), Cognitive Studies: Deficits in Cognition, pp. 280–323. Brunner/Mazel Publishers, New York.

Menyuk, P. 1971. The Acquisition and Development of Language. Prentice-Hall Inc., Englewood Cliffs, N. J.

Menyuk, P. 1974. The bases of language acquisition: Some questions. J. Autism and Child. Schizo. 4(4):325–345.

Moore, P. 1976. Art and the autistic child. Arts and Activities 79:28–30.

Mordock, J. B. 1970. Recent innovations in teaching the autistic child. Forum 6(1):3–13.

National Society for Autistic Children. 1973. National Information and Referral Service for Autistic and Autistic-like Persons. National Society for Autistic Children, Inc., Albany, N. Y.

Ornitz, E. M. 1973. Childhood autism, a review of the clinical and experimental literature. West. J. Med. 118:21–47.

Ornitz, E. M. 1974. The modulation of sensory input and motor output in autistic children. J. Autism Child. Schizo. 4:197–215.

Park, C. C. 1967. The Siege. Harcourt, Brace & World, Inc., New York.

Park, D. 1975. The development of infantile autism. NSAC Newsletter 7:17. National Society for Autistic Children, Inc., Albany, N.Y.

Parten, M. 1932. Social participation among preschool children. J. Abnorm. Soc. Psychol. 27:243–269.

Piaget, J. 1952. The Origins of Intelligence in Children. International Universities Press Inc., New York.

Piaget, J. 1954. The Construction of Reality in the Child. Basic Books Inc., New York.

Piaget, J. 1959. Judgment and Reasoning in the Child. Littlefield, Adams & Co., Patterson, N.J.

Piaget, J. 1967. Six Psychological Studies. Random House Inc., New York.

Rappaport, D. 1960. Psychoanalysis as a developmental psychology. *In* B. Kaplan and S. Wapner (eds.), Perspectives in Psychological Theory, pp. 209–255. International Universities Press Inc., New York.

Redl, F. 1959. The concept of therapeutic milieu. Am. J. Orthopsychiatry 29:721–727.

Rimland, B. 1964. Infantile Autism: The Syndrome and Its Implications for a Neutral Theory of Behavior. Appleton-Century-Crofts Inc. New York.

Ritvo, E. R. (ed.). 1976. Autism: Diagnosis, Current Research and Management. Spectrum Publications, New York.

Ritvo, E. R., Cantwell, D., Johnson, E., Clements, M., Benbrook, F., Slagle S., Kelly, P., and Ritz, M. 1971. Social class factors in autism. J. Autism Child. Schizo. 1(3):297–310.

Ruttenberg, B., and Wolf, E. G. 1967. Evaluating the communication of the autistic child. J. Speech Hear. 32:314–324.

Rutter, M. 1965. Speech disorders in a series of autistic children. *In* A. W. Franklin (ed.), Children with Communication Problems, pp. 39–47. Pitman Medical Publishing Co., London.

Rutter, M. 1968. Coincepts of autism: A review of research. J. Child Psychology 9:1–25.

Rutter, M. 1970. Autistic children: Infancy to adulthood. Semin. Psychiatry 2:435–450.

Rutter, M. 1970. The description and classification of infantile autism. Proceedings of the Indiana University colloquium on infantile autism. Charles C Thomas, Springfield, Ill.

Rutter, M., and Sussewein, F. 1971. A developmental and behavioral approach to the treatment of preschool autistic children. J. Autism Child. Schizo. 1:376–397.

Schopler, E. 1965. Early infantile autism and receptor processes. Arch. Gen. Psychiatry 13:327–335.

Schopler, E., and Reichler, R. J. 1971. Parents as cotherapists in the treatment of psychotic children. J. Autism Child. Schizo. 1:87–102.

Sears, R. R., Rau, L., and Alpert, R. 1965. Identification and Child Rearing. Stanford University Press, Stanford.

Shapiro, E., and Biber, B. 1973. The education of young children: A developmental-interaction approach. *In* S. G. Sapir and A. C. Nitzburg (eds.), Children with Learning Problems, pp. 682–709. Brunner/Mazel Publishers, New York.

Stuecher, U. 1972. Tommy: Treatment study of an autistic child. Council for Exceptional Children, Reston, Va.

Swan, W. W. 1971. The development of an observational instrument based on the objectives of developmental therapy. Unpublished doctoral dissertation. University of Georgia, College of Education.

Swan, W. W., and Wood, M. M. 1975. Making decisions about treatment effectiveness. *In* M. M. Wood (ed.), Developmental Therapy, pp. 37–59. University Park Press, Baltimore.

Thomas, A., and Chess, S. 1977. Temperament and Development. Brunner/Mazel Publishers, New York.

Treffert, D. A. 1970. Epidemiology of infantile autism. Arch. Gen. Psychiatry 22:431–438.

Turiel, E. 1969. Developmental processes in the child's moral thinking. *In* P. Mussen, J. Langer, and M. Covington (eds.), Trends and Issues in Developmental Psychology, pp. 92–133. Holt, Rinehart & Winston, New York.

Williams, A. 1975. The stage one class: A place for responding and trusting. *In* M. M. Wood (ed.), Developmental Therapy, pp. 157–174. University Park Press, Baltimore.

Williams, G. H., and Wood, M. M. 1977. Developmental Art Therapy. University Park Press, Baltimore.

Wing, J. K. 1966. Childhood Autism: Clinical, Educational and Social Aspects. Pergamon Press, Oxford.

Wing, L. 1972. Autistic children: A Guide for Parents and Professionals. Brunner/Mazel Publishers, New York.

Wing, L. 1974. Children Apart, Autistic Children and Their Families. National Society for Autistic Children, Inc., Albany, N.Y.

Wolff, P. H. 1960. The developmental psychologies of Jean Piaget and psychoanalysis. Psychol. Issues 2:40–181.

Wolff, S., and Chess, S. 1965. An analysis of the language of 14 schizophrenic children. J. Child Psychol. Psychiatry 6:29.

Wood, M. M. (ed.). 1972. The Rutland Center Model for Teaching Emotionally Disturbed Children. Eric No. ED 087703. Rutland Center Technical Assistance Office, Athens, Ga.

Wood, M. M. 1975. A developmental curriculum for social and emotional growth. *In* D. Lillie (ed.), Early Childhood Education: An Individualized Approach to Developmental Instruction. Science Research Associates Inc., Chicago.

Zigler, E., and Child, I. L. 1969. Socialization. *In* G. Lindzey and E. Aronson, (eds.), Handbook of Social Psychology, Vol. 3. Addison-Wesley Publishing Company Inc., New York.

Index

Academic objectives at Stages One
and Two in Developmental
Therapy, 156–160
    activities for mastery of, 66,
77–85, 90–92, 125–126,
137–139, 141
    criteria for identifying mastery of,
53–54
    goals of, 54
    tracking of, 58
Academics, as Developmental Therapy curriculum area, 58
    assessment of, 53–54
Activities, in Developmental Therapy
program, 17–18
    core activities, 20–24
    steps within, 18–20
    see also Learning experiences
Activity cards, for use in home
programs, 35, 37–39, 42
Art time, 17
    learning experiences, 120–126
Autism, incidence of, 4
Autistic children
    characteristics of, 3
    defined, 3
    see also CSID children

Bathroom time, 17
    learning experiences, 114–115
Behavior, as Developmental Therapy
curriculum area, 6, 55
    assessment of, 47–49
Behavior objectives at Stages One
and Two in Development
Therapy, 144–147

activities for mastery of, 61–63,
69–70, 87, 107–108, 111,
115, 117–118, 121,
129–133
criteria for identifying mastery of,
48–49
emphasis of, 53
tracking of, 55

Commands, as technique in Developmental Therapy activities,
25
Communication
    as Developmental Therapy curri-
culum area, 6, 56
        assessment of, 50–51
    sound, types of, 50
Communication objectives at Stage
One and Two in Develop-
mental Therapy, 148–150
    activities for mastery of, 71,
95–96, 99–101, 113,
122–124, 134–135
    and Music Time, 24
    criteria for identifying mastery of,
50–51
    tracking of, 56
Controlled vocabulary, as technique
in Developmental Therapy
activities, 24–25, 26
CSID children
    characteristics of, 8, 20, 25
    communication of, 50
    defined, 3
    developmental curriculum for, 3–4

difficulties in rating, 47
identifying developmental needs
    of, 17
problems of, 17
see also Autistic children

Dance time, 17
    learning experiences, 106–108
Developmental Therapy
    curriculum and classes, 6–7, 17,
20
        areas, 20, 21
        developmental milestones in,
general scope and sequence
of, 54–58
    evaluation of program, 7–11
    explanation of program, 4–5
    illustration of child progress,
8–11
    and parallel school experiences,
6
    parent involvement in, 5–6
        field experiences, 5–6
        home programs, 6, 27–42
        observation, 5
        specific skill development pro-
gram, 5
    planning a program, 17–20
    referrals for, of children, 5
    stages of, 7
    techniques to use in activities,
24–26
Developmental Therapy curriculum
objectives for Stages One
and Two, 143–160
    comments about, 45–58
    see also specific curriuclum areas

183

Developmental Therapy Objectives
Rating Form (DTORF), 7,
8, 17, 29, 47, 161–164
sample summary, 8, 9–10, 175
DTORF, *see* Developmental Therapy
Objectives Rating Form

Echoing, as technique in Developmental Therapy activities,
25
Exercise time, 17, 44
learning experiences, 86–92

Feeding skills, learning of, 49
Field experiences, in Developmental
Therapy program, 5–6

Good-bye time, 17
learning experiences, 140–141

Hello time, 17, 18
learning experiences, 68–74
Home programs, 6
for a cerebral palsied, nonambulatory child, 30
designed around music activities,
32
designed to improve self-help
skills, 40–42
implementing, 29
samples of, 27–44
to stimulate speech, 35–39
substitute program conducted by
day care staff, 43–44

Individualized Education Program
(IEP), 17, 165–175
Intake, as part of referral process, 5
Intervention, types of, in Develop-
mental programs, 7

Juice and cookies time, 31, 44
see also Snack time

Labeling
by adult, to increase awareness in
CSID child, 22

by child, as indicative of progress
in communication objec-
tives, 50, 51
Language, as focus in Developmental
Therapy activities, 22
Language stimulation program, 35
Learning experiences, samples of,
59–141
art time, 120–126
bathroom time, 114–115
dance time, 106–108
exercise time, 86–92
good-bye time, 140–141
hello time, 68–74
music time, 128–139
outside time, 110–111
play time, 60–66
sand or water time, 116–118
snack time, 112–113
story time, 98–104
work time, 76–85
yum-yum time, 94–96
see also Activities
Life Space Interviewing (LSI), 7

Objectives, *see* Developmental Therapy curriculum objectives
for Stages One and Two
Observation, by parents, in Developmental Therapy program, 5
Outside time, 17
learning experiences, 110–111

Milk and cookies time, *see* Snack
time
Motor skills, importance of, for child
in learning, 53
Music program, as Developmental
Therapy home program,
33–34
Music time, 17, 23–24
learning experiences, 128–139

Parallel play, 53
Parallel school program, 6
Parallel talk, 36

Parents
as co-teacher, 4, 5, 25
role of
in Developmental Therapy
stages, 7
in home programs, 29
see also Developmental Therapy, parent involvement
skill development program for, 5
Parent training sequence, 5
Physical intervention, as technique in
Developmental Therapy ac-
tivities, 26
Play time, 17, 20–22, 31, 44
learning experiences, 60–66
(Pre)Academics
as Developmental Therapy curriculum area, 6
see also Academics

Redirection, 7, 26
Referral Form Checklist (RFCL), 8
Referrals, to Developmental Therapy
program, 5
Reflecting statements, as technique
in Developmental Therapy
activities, 25
RFCL, *see* Referral Form Checklist
Routine, importance of, at Stage One
in Developmental Therapy,
18
Rutland Center, Athens, Georgia, 3,
4–5, 165

Sand time, 17
learning experience, 118
Schedule, for Stage One class, 17–20
School program, as parallel to Developmental Therapy program,
6
Screening, as part of referral process,
5
Self-help skills, learning of, 40–42,
49
Sensory channels, of child, 47
Skill development program, for parents, 5
Snack time, 17, 22–23
learning experiences, 112–113